WOMEN OF WORDS

SECOND EDITION

A PERSONAL INTRODUCTION TO MORE THAN FORTY IMPORTANT WRITERS

Edited by Janet Bukovinsky Teacher

Portraits by Jenny Powell

RUNNING PRESS

PHILADELPHIA · LONDON

9   8   7   6   5   4   3   2   I
Digit on the right indicates the number of this printing

Library of Congress Cataloging-in-Publication Number 2001087046

ISBN 0-7624-1078-7

Picture research by Jane Sanders
Cover and interior design by Nancy Loggins and Serrin Bodmer
Edited by Greg Aaron and Sara Phillips
Typography: Centaur MT by Deborah Luger

This book may be ordered by mail from the publisher.
Please include $2.50 for postage and handling.
But try your bookstore first!

Running Press Book Publishers
125 South Twenty-second Street
Philadelphia, Pennsylvania 19103-4399

Visit us on the web!
www.runningpress.com

Contents

Introduction

A pen scratches against paper in the diffused glow of an oil lamp. The children are soundly asleep, the parents, sisters, husband long since gone to bed. With a shawl around her shoulders against the chill of the night, a woman hunches at a table, turning over page after page into a neat pile. She writes rapidly, in cadence with her thoughts, pausing only to dip her pen back into the inkwell.

It was through such solitary labor, whether pursued with foolscap and ink, manual typewriter, or the technical marvel of a word processor, that the thirty-five women profiled in this book achieved their goals. Stealing time was an essential skill for creative women of the eighteenth and nineteenth centuries, and remains so today. Time has always been a great luxury for women, the traditional housekeepers and family caretakers, and only in quiet hours was the peace and concentration necessary for writing to be found. The exceptions, of course, were women like Charlotte Brontë and Willa Cather, who chose not to marry or have families, but still needed to support themselves. Such women may have become masters of their own creative fates, but finding the time to create was only half the battle.

Ask anyone who makes a living with words: writing is hard work. To be a writer is not nearly as significant an achievement as is the act of having written something fine and eloquent. Those who think they might enjoy or even excel at such a pursuit—if only they could find the time—would do well to take their inspiration from the women gathered in these pages. They didn't let housework, depression, childbirth, war, madness, disapproval, or poverty stand in their ways. They wrote, most of them, simply because the urge to share some cautionary tale, make an observation, or state facts in compelling new ways was so strong. And the worlds to which they brought their readers ranged from the prim drawing-rooms of Jane Austen's British countryside to the extraterrestrial empires of Ursula K. Le Guin to the close-knit African-American communities of Nobel Prize winner Toni Morrison.

Some of the women whose work appears in *Women of Words* did become writers out of economic need: Kate Chopin, a young widow with six children, turned her flair for creating stories into a viable means of supporting her family. Others, like Jane Austen and Edith Wharton, chafed under the stiff, high collar of privilege, escaping the hothouse atmospheres of their limited lives by spinning tales of romance, intrigue, or morals. Though Wharton's meticulous rendering of New York City's late nineteenth-century high society makes such books as *The Age of Innocence* seem like photo albums of a time gone by, the relationships between men, women, friends, and families remain as relevant today as they were during the stilted, gilded 1870s.

Morality and politics fueled some of these women's literary aspirations. Sadness, occasionally, was also a factor. The novelist Elizabeth Gaskell wrote her first book, a scathing indictment of mid-nineteenth-century factory life and the plight of the working man, to divert herself from the death of an infant son. The earliest author included herein, Mary Wollstonecraft, took it upon herself to instruct readers in the moral education of children, a popular topic of conversation among women in the late eighteenth century. However, she also wrote with previously unseen fervor about the inequality of women's position in society, a theme that was to be echoed and built upon by other writers, including the French feminist pioneer Simone de Beauvoir and the American Dorothy Parker, whose painfully honest works often contain the rueful observation that love—pure, true romantic ardor—seems to matter more to women than it does to men. Love lost or unrequited, or the heart's first frenzy of passion, has compelled many a woman to take up the pen.

While pursuing fiction, the mind does a dance of its own choosing, sometimes reeling off situations invented from sheer caprice. It is possible to invent scenes of incredible passion and pain and still appear as prim to the outside world as a nineteenth-century schoolmarm—a position held, as a matter of fact, by half a dozen of these women of words. Since decorum was, until recent decades, an expected womanly trait, the possibilities offered by the writing life could make the life of a sheltered writer quite an exciting one.

Ultimately, what inspired all these women were books. Some were the daughters of ministers, the men favored with education in their times. Others were fortunate enough to grow up in homes where books were the valued sources of great ideas. I hope that the small tastes of their creations contained herein will be an encouragement to seek out the works in their entireties, for *Women of Words* is meant to be a companion to anyone moved by the glorious breadth of literature by women. Wherever you open this book, you will meet a woman, read about her life, sample her work, and perhaps search for clues to her personality and motivations in the portraits which accompany each section.

In researching this book, and selecting the excerpts, I spent my evenings in the company of some fascinating characters, from the dashing explorer Denys Finch-Hatton, who wooed Isak Dinesen in *Out of Africa*, to the charming hostess Gertrude Stein, portrayed with such clever insight by none other then Miss Stein herself in *The Autobiography of Alice B. Toklas*. I read dozens and dozens of books. Still, that amounts to the smallest fraction of the volumes written by women all over the world who have had something to say and the wherewithal to see their notions put into print—a mere scratching of the surface, one might say. I console myself with the thought that scratching the surface, like the scratching of a pen against paper, or the ruminative tapping of a computer keyboard, at least amounts to a respectable beginning, and may just reveal a rich source of inspiration the deeper one ventures into the world of women's literature.

Mary Wollstonecraft

(1759–1797)

"Independence I have long considered as the grand blessing of life, the basis of every virtue." Boldly feminist for its time, the opinion rose from the inkwell of Mary Wollstonecraft. No English-speaking woman had ever been so audacious as to question the validity of marriage as she did, or to suggest that men might be preventing women from pursuing their rightful place in society.

The second of seven children, Wollstonecraft was born in London, but spent her youth moving throughout England and Wales at the whim of a brutish, hard-drinking father. (No doubt her parents' tumultuous relationship helped form Wollstonecraft's rather extreme notions about marriage later on.) She returned to London as a young adult and published first a novel for adults—considered scandalous at the time—entitled *Mary: A Fiction* (1788), and then a book for children, *Thoughts on the Education of Daughters* (1787). Though she had no children at the time, Wollstonecraft had occasion to observe their behavior in her work as a governess.

Soon, she began to write book reviews and translations for her publisher Joseph Johnson, a London bookseller. He promoted many of the era's progressive thinkers, including Wollstonecraft's colleagues Wordsworth and Cowper. Wollstonecraft became known for her acid-tongued literary reviews.

She further shocked Britain's reading public with radical views on abortion, divorce, and, most memorably, women's rights. Horace Walpole, a contemporary, went so far as to call her "a hyena in petticoats." She received this epithet for opinions expressed in her landmark treatise—now widely considered the first feminist work in modern English literature—*A Vindication of the Rights of Women* (1792). In it, she argued that women should be given the benefit of education. In part, Wollstonecraft's feminist ardor grew out of earlier considerations of human rights. The passionate politics of the French Revolution had previously inspired her to write about property ownership and personal freedom in *A Vindication of the Rights of Men* (1790).

After publication of *A Vindication of the Rights of Women*, Wollstonecraft moved to Paris, where she met Gilbert Imlay, an American writer, and bore his daughter, Fanny, out of wedlock. Imlay's neglect of her caused Mary to return to England and led her to twice attempt suicide. With the help of her sister, Wollstonecraft established a school at Newington Green. There she fell in love with William Godwin, a famous anarchical minister and founding member of the Unitarian Society.

Despite the disdain for marriage both had expressed in their writing, Wollstonecraft and Godwin wed in 1797, after she became pregnant again. She died shortly after giving birth to a second daughter, Mary Wollstonecraft Shelley. She left behind an uncompleted novel, *The Wrongs of Woman*, or *Maria*, about a woman and her faithless lover—a woman who, in her strengths and weaknesses, bears an uncanny resemblance to the passionate Mary Wollstonecraft herself.

In 1795, Wollstonecraft—already famous for her landmark works on women's rights and education—set out on a solitary journey to Scandinavia. The result was a book entitled A Short Residence in Sweden, Norway, and Denmark *(1796), written in letter form. Here, Wollstonecraft's observations of the trip are interwoven with her melancholy over missing her young child, whom she left behind in England. She also refers sadly to her friend Fanny Blood, who died in Portugal the previous year.*

A woman, coming alone, interested the Norwegians. And I know not whether my weariness gave me a look of peculiar delicacy; but they approached to assist me, and enquire after my wants, as if they were afraid to hurt, and wished to protect me. The sympathy I inspired, thus dropping down from the clouds in a strange land, affected me more than it would have done, had not my spirits been harassed by various causes—by much thinking—musing almost to madness—and even by a sort of weak melancholy that hung about my heart at parting with my daughter for the first time.

You know that as a female I am particularly attached to her—I feel more than a mother's fondness and anxiety, when I reflect on the dependent and oppressed state of her sex. I dread lest she should be forced to sacrifice her heart to her principles, or principles to her heart. With trembling hand I shall cultivate sensibility, and cherish delicacy of sentiment, lest, whilst I lend fresh blushes to the rose, I sharpen the thorns that will wound the breast I would fain guard—I dread to unfold her mind, lest it should render her unfit for the world she is to inhabit—Hapless woman! what a fate is thine!

But whither am I wandering? I only meant to tell you that the impression the kindness of the

Mary Wollstonecraft

simple people made visible on my countenance increased my sensibility to a painful degree. I wished to have had a room to myself; for their attention, and rather distressing observation, embarrassed me extremely. Yet, as they would bring me eggs, and make my coffee, I found I could not leave them without hurting their feelings of hospitality.

It is customary here for the host and hostess to welcome their guests as master and mistress of the house.

My clothes, in their turn, attracted the attention of the females; and I could not help thinking of the foolish vanity which makes many women so proud of the observation of strangers as to take wonder very gratuitously for admiration. This error they are very apt to fall into; when arrived in a foreign country, the populace stare at them as they pass; yet the make of a cap, or the singularity of a gown, is often the cause of the flattering attention, which afterwards supports a fantastic superstructure of self-conceit.

Not having brought a carriage over with me, expecting to have met a person where I landed, who was immediately to have procured me one, I was detained whilst the good people of the inn sent round to all their acquaintance to search for a vehicle. . . .

I had to pass over, I was informed, the most fertile and best cultivated tract of country in Norway. The distance was three Norwegian miles, which are longer than the Swedish. The roads were very good; the farmers obliged to repair them; and we scampered through a great extent of country in a more improved state than any I had viewed since I left England. Still there was sufficient of hills, dales, and rocks, to prevent the idea of a plain from entering the head, or even of such scenery as England and France afford. The prospects were also embellished by water, rivers, and lakes, before the sea proudly claimed my regard; and the road running frequently through lofty groves, rendered the landscapes beautiful, though they were not so romantic as those I had lately seen with such delight.

It was late when I reached Tønsberg; and I was glad to go to bed at a decent inn. The next morning, the 17 July, conversing with the gentlemen with whom I had business to transact, I found that I should be detained at Tønsberg three weeks; and I lamented that I had not brought my child with me.

The inn was quiet, and my room so pleasant, commanding a view of the sea, confined by an amphitheatre of hanging woods, that I wished to remain there, though no one in the house could speak English or French. The mayor, my friend, however, sent a young woman to me who spoke a little English, and she agreed to call on me twice a day, to receive orders, and translate them to my hostess.

My not understanding the language was an excellent pretext for dining alone, which I prevailed on them to let me do at a late hour; for the early dinners in Sweden had entirely deranged my day. I could not alter it there, without disturbing the economy of a family where I was a visitor; necessity having forced me to accept of an invitation from a private family, the lodgings were so incommodious.

Amongst the Norwegians I had the arrangement of my own time; and I determined to regulate it in such a manner, that I might enjoy as much of their sweet summer as I possibly could;—short, it is true; but "passing sweet."

I never endured a winter in this rude clime; consequently it was not the contrast, but the real beauty of the season which made the present summer appear to me the finest I had ever seen. Sheltered from the north and eastern winds, nothing can exceed the salubrity, the soft freshness of the western gales. In the evening they also die away; the aspen leaves tremble into stillness, and reposing nature seems to be warmed by the moon, which here assumes a genial aspect: and if a light shower has chanced to fall with the sun, the juniper the underwood of the forest, exhales a wild perfume, mixed with a thousand nameless sweets, that, soothing the heart, leave images in the memory which the imagination will ever hold dear.

Nature is the nurse of sentiment,—the true source of taste;—yet what misery, as well as rapture, is produced by a quick perception of the beautiful and sublime, when it is exercised in observing animated nature, when every beauteous feeling and emotion excites responsive sympathy, and the harmonized soul sinks into melancholy, or rises to extasy, just as the chords are touched, like the aeolian harp agitated by the changing wind. But how dangerous is it to foster these sentiments in such an imperfect state of existence; and how difficult to eradicate them when an affection for mankind, a passion for an individual, is but the unfolding of that love which embraces all that is great and beautiful.

When a warm heart has received strong impressions, they are not to be effaced. Emotions become sentiments; and the imagination renders even transient sensations permanent, by fondly retracing them. I cannot, without a thrill of delight, recollect views I have seen, which are not to be forgotten,—nor looks I have felt in every nerve which I shall never more meet. The grave has closed over a dear friend, the friend of my youth; still she is present with me, and I hear her soft voice warbling as I stray over the heath. Fate has separated me from another, the fire of whose eyes, tempered by infantine tenderness, still warms my breast; even when gazing on these tremendous cliffs, sublime emotions absorb my soul. And, smile not, if I add, that the rosy tint of morning reminds me of a suffusion, which will never more charm my senses, unless it reappears on the cheeks of my child. Her sweet blushes I may yet hide in my bosom, and she is still too young to ask why starts the tear, so near akin to the pleasure and pain?

Jane Austen

(1775–1817)

The sixth of seven children, born in Steventon, Hampshire, young Jane Austen was taught to read and write by her father, a prosperous minister. But while her contemporaries Wordsworth and Coleridge were out in the world, studying at Cambridge University, Austen's entire education took place inside the family parlor. There she visited with friends, wrote letters, and read voraciously, everything from Shakespeare to Fanny Burney. Austen was acutely aware of her condition. "Men have had every advantage of us in telling their own story," She wrote. "Education has been theirs in so much higher a degree; the pen has been in their hands."

Fond of long walks in the countryside—her novels frequently feature the independent vision of a woman walking alone in some bucolic setting—Austen lived most of her life surrounded by family members in Steventon, Bath, and Chawton. It is said that she disdained both her parents, particularly her father. Critics have long pointed out the preoccupation with money evident in her works. Ralph Waldo Emerson went so far as to call it "vulgar."

Like many women of the time, Austen believed the primary concern of a young woman ought to be her marriageability. She begins her most famous work, *Pride and Prejudice* (1813) with this statement: "It is a truth universally acknowledged that a single man in possession of a good fortune must be in want of a wife." In fact, one scholar has pointed out that *all* of Austen's opening paragraphs contain a mention of finances. Though her heroines flirt outrageously, they remain dignified and manage to snare a husband before it's too late. Ironically, Austen herself never wed. She once accepted a suitor's offer, only to change her mind the next morning. All in all, Austen's life was remarkably quiet and uneventful.

That is, except for her devotion to writing. By the age of fourteen, Austen had already

Jane Austen

completed a novelette entitled *Love and Friendship*, gently spoofing a heroine who rejects her parents' love and support. "I think I may boast myself to be, with all possible vanity, the most unlearned and uninformed female who ever dared to be an authoress," Jane wrote. But she persevered, and eventually there came the masterful *Pride and Prejudice* (1813), set in a rarefied world of front parlors and grand ballrooms, full of whispers, deceptions, and affectations. She changed the subject from courtship to clerical ordination in *Mansfield Park* (1814), a sort of morality play about entering the church, in which the truly good heroine competes with a dazzling, witty rival for the attentions of a man they both love. The heroine triumphs, while the book criticizes social conventions and falsehoods. *Emma* (1816) chronicles how a spoiled young heiress—not an especially appealing character—fritters away her time and misbehaves until she learns a valuable lesson about respecting the tenant farmers who manage her land. Austen's descriptions of the lives of carpenters and dairymaids, modeled after characters in her own life, are realistic and informative.

Persuasion* and *Northanger Abbey* were published after Austen's death in 1817. The latter combines a satire of contemporary gothic novels with an enchanting romantic comedy about the elaborate mating rituals of the time. Austen was working on *Sanditon*, another novel, when she died.

The pursuit, rejection, and achievement of a financially rewarding marriage by the five Bennet sisters in a central concern in Pride and Prejudice, *a novel of manners and class consciousness written in 1813. Here, Lydia is preparing to marry her highly unsuitable suitor, George Wickham, whose proposal had just been rejected by her sister Elizabeth.*

Their sister's wedding day arrived; and Jane and Elizabeth felt for her probably more than she felt for herself. The carriage was sent to meet them at———, and they were to return in it by dinner-time. Their arrival was dreaded by the elder Miss Bennets; and Jane more especially, who gave Lydia the feelings, which would have attended herself, had *she* been the culprit, was wretched in the thought of what her sister must endure.

They came. The family were assembled in the breakfast-room to receive them. Smiles decked the face of Mrs. Bennet as the carriage drove up to the door; her husband looked impenetrably grave; her daughters alarmed, anxious, uneasy.

Lydia's voice was heard in the vestibule; the door was thrown open, and she ran into the room. Her mother stepped forwards, embraced her, and welcomed her with rapture; gave her hand with an affectionate smile to Wickham, who followed his lady, and wished them both joy, with an alacrity which showed no doubt of their happiness.

Their reception from Mr. Bennet, to whom they then turned, was not quite so cordial. His countenance rather gained in austerity; and he scarcely opened his lips. The easy assurance of the young couple, indeed, was enough to provoke him. Elizabeth was disgusted, and even Miss Bennet was shocked. Lydia was Lydia still; untamed, unabashed, wild, noisy, and fearless. She turned from sister to sister, demanding their congratulations, and when at length they all sat down, looked eagerly round the room, took notice of some little alteration in it, and observed, with a laugh, that it was a great while since she had been there.

Wickham was not at all more distressed than herself, but his manners were always so pleasing that had his character and his marriage been exactly what they ought, his smiles and his easy address, while he claimed their relationship, would have delighted them all. Elizabeth had not before believed him quite equal to such assurance; but she sat down, resolving within herself to draw no limits in future to the impudence of an impudent man. *She* blushed, and Jane blushed; but the cheeks of the two who caused their confusion suffered no variation of colour.

There was no want of discourse. The bride and her mother could neither of them talk fast enough; and Wickham, who happened to sit near Elizabeth, began inquiring after his acquaintance in that neighbourhood with a good-humoured ease, which she felt very unable to equal in her replies. They seemed each of them to have the happiest memories in the world. Nothing of the past was recollected with pain; and Lydia led voluntarily to subjects which her sisters would not have alluded to for the world.

"Only think of its being three months," she cried, "since I went away; it seems but a fortnight I declare; and yet there have been things enough happened in the time. Good gracious! when I went away, I am sure I had no more idea of being married till I came back again! though I thought it would be very good fun if I was."

Her father lifted up his eyes. Jane was distressed, Elizabeth looked expressively at Lydia; but she, who never heard nor saw anything of which she chose to be insensible, gaily continued, "Oh! Mamma, do the people here abouts know I am married to-day? I was afraid they might not; and we overtook William Goulding in his curricle, so I was determined he should know it, and so I let down the side glass next to him, and took off my glove, and let my hand just rest upon the window frame, so that he might see the ring, and then I bowed and smiled like anything."

Elizabeth could bear it no longer. She got up, and ran out of the room; and returned no more, till she heard them passing through the hall to the dining-parlour. She then joined them soon' enough to see Lydia, with anxious parade, walk up to her mother's right hand, and hear her say to her eldest sister, "Ah! Jane, I take your place now, and you must go lower, because I am a married woman."

It was not to be supposed that time would give Lydia that embarrassment from which she had been so wholly free at first. Her ease and good spirits increased. She longed to see Mrs. Philips, the Lucases, and all their other neighbours, and to hear herself called "Mrs. Wickham" by each of them; and in the meantime, she went after dinner to show her ring and boast of being married to Mrs. Hill and the two housemaids.

"Well, Mamma," said she, when they were

all returned to the breakfast-room, "and what do you think of my husband? Is not he a charming man? I am sure my sisters must all envy me. I only hope they may have half my good luck. They must all go to Brighton. That is the place to get husbands. What a pity it is, Mamma, we did not all go."

"Very true; and if I had my will, we should. But my dear Lydia, I don't at all like your going such a way off. Must it be so?"

"Oh, lord! yes; there is nothing in that. I shall like it of all things. You and Papa, and my sisters, must come down and see us. We shall be at Newcastle all the winter, and I dare say there will be some balls, and I will take care to get good partners for them all."

"I should like it beyond anything!" said her mother.

"And then when you go away, you may leave one or two of my sisters behind you; and I dare say I shall get husbands for them before the winter is over."

"I thank you for my share of the favour," said Elizabeth; "but I do not particularly like your way of getting husbands."

Mary Wollstonecraft Shelley

(1797–1851)

Mary Wollstonecraft Shelley created a monster. Her most famous work, *Frankenstein*, is a science fiction classic that resulted from a writing exercise intended to pass the time one rainy afternoon in 1816. She was on holiday with her fiancé, Percy Bysshe Shelley, and their friend Lord Byron. All three writers had been reading and discussing Gothic ghost stories and agreed to give the genre a try. The two men did not finish their tales, but Mary did. Later, she wrote that the plot had come to her in a nightmare. It presaged an eerie time, for in the months that followed, both her half sister (Lord Byron's lover) and Shelley's estranged wife committed suicide.

Bright and accomplished, Mary Godwin was raised by an intellectual father and his second wife. Her mother, the writer Mary Wollstonecraft, died shortly after giving birth. As a child, Mary learned Greek, Latin, and other languages, and read Coleridge and Wordsworth. Looking back, she wrote, "As a child I scribbled. . . . Still I had a dearer pleasure than this, which was the formation of castles in the air."

She became pregnant at age 16, after falling in love with Percy Shelley, and was almost constantly pregnant for the next five years, though only one son survived. Mary's traumatic experiences with motherhood, scholars believe, account for her creation of a literary birth myth. Still, she brought birth to fiction not as a realistic part of a woman's life, but as a tragic fantasy, that of the alienated scientist who locks himself in a laboratory. He is convinced that he had discovered the heady secret to creating life, only to discover that the results of tampering with nature can be hideous.

The story of that scientist, *Frankenstein* (1818), is told through the device of letters to Walton, an English explorer in the Arctic. Mary made the monster's birth a thing of horror,

Mary Wollstonecraft Shelley

and Frankenstein, a student of natural philosophy, never even gives it a name. In fact, he abandons the piteous, confused creature, who turns on him, murdering his wife, brother, and colleague. In a frenzy for revenge, Frankenstein pursues the monster to the Arctic. Both the creator and his creation perish in the waste.

In addition to other novels, biographies, and short stories, many published in *The Keepsake* magazine, Shelley wrote *Rambles in Germany and Italy* while she was abroad in the early 1840s. Her journals contain detailed accounts of the books she read, but surprisingly make few mentions of her numerous pregnancies. She did, however, continue putting elements of Gothic fiction and science fiction into her works. In *The Last Man* her protagonist is a young shepherd who grows up and finds himself the last person alive in the plague-ravaged year 2100.

After her husband's passing in 1822, Mary returned to England. There she edited his poems and letters. As Frankenstein said when he studied the decaying corpse from which he created life: "To examine the causes of life, we must first have recourse to death." By passing on her visions, and those of her husband, she greatly enriched the lives of countless readers.

In Shelley's famous Gothic horror story, Doctor Frankenstein is both enervated and exhilarated by the awesome range of his power as he collects the raw materials to be used in the creation of his horrific new species.

When I found so astonishing a power placed within my hands, I hesitated a long time concerning the manner in which I should employ it. Although I possessed the capacity of bestowing animation, yet to prepare a frame for the reception of it, with all its intricacies of fibres, muscles, and veins, still remained a work of inconceivable difficulty and labour. I doubted at first whether I should attempt the creation of a being like myself, or one of simpler organization; but my imagination was too much exalted by my first success to permit me to doubt of my ability to give life to an animal as complex and wonderful as man. The materials at present within my command hardly appeared adequate to so arduous an undertaking, but I doubted not that I should ultimately succeed. I prepared myself for a multitude of reverses; my operations might be incessantly baffled, and at last my work be imperfect, yet when I considered the improvement which every day takes place in science and mechanics, I was encouraged to hope my present attempts would at least lay the foundations of future success. Nor could I consider the magnitude and complexity of my plan as any argument of its impracticability. It was with these feelings that I began the creation of a human being. As the minuteness of the parts formed a great hindrance to my speed, I resolved, contrary to my first intention, to make the being of a gigantic stature, that is to say, about eight feet in height, and proportionably large. After having formed this determination and having spent some months in successfully collecting and arranging my materials, I began.

No one can conceive the variety of feelings which bore me onwards, like a hurricane, in the first enthusiasm of success. Life and death appeared to me ideal bounds, which I should first break through, and pour a torrent of light into our dark world. A new species would bless me as its creator and source; many happy and excellent natures would owe their being to me. No father could claim the gratitude of his child so completely as I should deserve theirs. Pursuing these reflections, I thought that if I could bestow animation upon lifeless matter, I might in process of time (although I now found it impossible) renew life where death had apparently devoted the body to corruption.

These thoughts supported my spirits, while I pursued my undertaking with unremitting ardour. My cheek had grown pale with study, and my person had become emaciated with confinement. Sometimes, on the very brink of certainty, I failed; yet still I clung to the hope which the next day or the next hour might realize. One secret which I alone possessed was the hope to which I had dedicated myself; and the moon gazed on my midnight labours, while, with unrelaxed and breathless eagerness, I pursued nature to her hiding-places. Who shall conceive the horrors of my secret toil as I dabbled among the unhallowed damps of the grave or tortured the living animal to animate the lifeless clay? My limbs now tremble, and my eyes swim with the remembrance; but then a resistless and almost frantic impulse urged me forward; I seemed to have lost all soul or sensation but for this one pursuit. It was indeed but a passing trance, that only made me feel with renewed acuteness so soon as, the unnatural stimulus ceasing to operate, I had returned to my old habits. I collected bones from charnel-houses and disturbed, with profane fingers, the tremendous secrets of the human frame. In a solitary chamber, or rather cell, at the top of the house, and separated from all the other apartments by a gallery and staircase, I kept my workshop of filthy creation; my eyeballs were starting from their sockets in attending to the details of my employment. The dissecting room and the slaughter-house furnished many of my materials; and often did my human nature turn with loathing from my occupation, whilst, still urged on by an eagerness which perpetually increased, I brought my work near to a conclusion.

Elizabeth Barrett Browning

(1806–1861)

"**I** heard an angel speak last night,/ And he said, 'Write!'" Thus Elizabeth Barrett Browning described the passion that sustained her throughout a difficult life and assured her a position as one of the nineteenth century's most beloved writers.

Prior to her union with the writer Robert Browning at the spinsterish age of 40—immortalized in reams of lushly romantic verse, including *Sonnets from the Portuguese*—Barrett lived quietly in London and the British countryside. She was the eldest of her eleven siblings, born to a mother most often described as meek, and a strict father who had made his fortune in Jamaican plantations. Barrett was educated primarily at home, and largely of her own volition. She corresponded with a number of prominent writers and scholars, studied the classics, and published translations of Greek and Byzantine verse.

Despite the privileges of her world, Barrett knew sorrow on intimate terms. In 1838, she nearly died of a broken blood vessel and was sent to recuperate at the seaside resort of Torquay. Two years later, her brother Edward drowned there while visiting. Barrett, wracked with grief, fled back to the family home in London. Even when she fell in love with Browning—an ardor that developed over the course of a year-long literary correspondence inspired by his admiration of her 1844 volume, titled *Poems*—she encountered obstacles. Her imperious father had forbidden any of his children to marry, so Barrett was forced to meet, come to know, and wed Browning in secret. Not surprisingly, the couple chose to move after their marriage. They set up housekeeping in Florence, Italy, where their child, Robert, was born in 1849.

In Italy, Barrett could finally enjoy happiness with an intellectual peer, and a social circle that included Ruskin, Tennyson, Hawthorne, Thackeray, Carlyle, and other estimable

Elizabeth Barrett Browning

contemporaries. She became intensely interested in Italian politics, spiritualism, and children's literature.

Barrett held progressive social opinions. In her poems, she also bucked tradition through her daring use of unorthodox forms of meter and versification. Despite the unusual aspects of her poetry, she was held in higher critical esteem as a writer, during her lifetime, than her husband was in his. Barrett's work met with greater commercial success and is acknowledged to be more accessible, even to this day.

Since their publication in 1850, her lyrical *Sonnets from the Portuguese* have been quoted by countless lovers. But Barrett's true magnum opus was *Aurora Leigh*, an 11,000-line "novel in verse" about the tumultuous life of a writer not unlike herself. The painstakingly crafted poem-story is set in a lush and gorgeous landscape, and is enhanced by the author's witty observations on the position of women in society. She comments with similar pithy insight on social issues. Barrett published several additional books of verse, political essays, and poems for children; and numerous volumes of her correspondence were issued after her death at the age of fifty-five.

Her deep affection for her husband during the early years of her marriage prompted Browning to write Sonnets from the Portuguese, *a collection of 44 love poems which have endured to this day as moving romantic tributes. The title was intended to hide the true subject of the poems by implying that they had been translated from some other source.*

XLIII

How do I love thee? Let me count the ways.
I love thee to the depth and breadth and height
My soul can reach, when feeling out of sight
For the ends of Being and ideal Grace.
I love thee to the level of everyday's
Most quiet need, by sun and candle-light.
I love thee freely, as men strive for Right;
I love thee purely, as they turn from Praise.
I love thee with the passion put to use
In my old griefs, and with my childhood's faith.
I love thee with a love I seemed to lose
With my lost saints,—I love thee with the breath,
Smiles, tears, of all my life!—and, if God choose,
I shall but love thee better after death.

XIV

If thou must love me, let it be for nought
Except for love's sake only. Do not say
"I love her for her smile—her look—her way
Of speaking gently,—for a trick of thought
That falls in well with mine, and certes brought
A sense of pleasant ease on such a day"—
For these things in themselves, Belovèd, may
Be changed, or change for thee,—and love, so wrought,
May be unwrought so. Neither love me for
Thine own dear pity's wiping my cheeks dry,—
A creature might forget to weep, who bore
Thy comfort long, and lose thy love thereby!
But love me for love's sake, that evermore
Thou mayst love on, through love's eternity.

Elizabeth Gaskell

(1810–1865)

In the tradition of women writers throughout history, Elizabeth Cleghorn Gaskell took time out of her busy life—wife of a Unitarian minister, mother of four daughters, gracious hostess—to put her thoughts on paper. She hinted in the preface of her best-known work, *Mary Barton: A Tale of Manchester Life* (1848) that a mysterious occurrence in her thirty-fifth year had prompted her to take a fresh and political turn in her work. This event, Gaskell's biographers now say, was the death of her infant son during the Hungry Forties, a time of political unrest in her native England. That turbulent period in pre-Industrial Revolution history provided the backdrop for this book, set in the grimy factory town of Manchester, her home.

As Elizabeth Cleghorn's own mother had died soon after childbirth, she was raised by an aunt and her father, also a Unitarian minister, as well as a journalist and politician. In 1832 she married William Gaskell and bore four daughters. She was said to have been a woman of exceptional physical beauty. Gaskell, whose circle of friends included Charles Dickens, Thomas Carlyle, Florence Nightingale, and John Ruskin, devoted much of her time to humanitarian causes and urged the improvement of communication between factory workers, who lived in poverty and squalor, and factory owners, the masters of the workers' fates.

Mary Barton was influenced by Charles Dickens's social activism and the unflinching literary realism of Jane Austen. Gaskell's work is rich with indigenous dialect, radical dogma, and heartfelt conversations between women and includes detailed scenes of workers' associations, economic upheavals, strikes, and bloody riots. All are seen through the eyes of a young woman in search of a husband, and an uneducated but sharp-witted workingman who sympathizes with the Chartists, members of a movement seeking social reform. In one

Elizabeth Gaskell

unforgettable scene, a worker dies of fever in a filthy basement, a death witnessed by family members who are themselves starving. The book's condemnation of employers so enraged some members of Gaskell's husband's congregation that they burned copies of it.

Gaskell's other novels include *Ruth* (1853), the story of a seduced and abandoned woman, and *Cranford* (1853), a series of quaint vignettes about country life, seen through the eagle eyes of a group of middle-aged women living in a Cheshire village. The latter was hailed during Gaskell's lifetime, but her other works—*North and South* (published serially in the 1850s), about a parson's daughter who finds a lover when she takes up with a mob of strikers, and *Sylvia's Lover*, a tale of romance and intrigue set in a northern England seaport during the Napoleonic era—received no critical acclaim until a century after her death.

Gaskell also wrote about thirty short stories and, in 1855, the first biography of her friend Charlotte Brontë. That book remains the most controversial Brontë biography, because it contained allegedly libelous statements which had to be corrected in future printings. Gaskell was at work on *Wives and Daughters* (1866), a family saga set in an English village, when she died of heart disease in the house she had bought for her husband's retirement with money she had earned as a writer.

Mary Barton was both a forerunner of today's political thrillers and a poignant tale of a daughter torn between parental devotion and a strong sense of right and wrong. In the scene that follows, Mary makes a startling discovery about her father, an impassioned activist whose involvement with a group of radical dissenters leads to tragedy.

No sooner was Mary alone than she fastened the door, and put the shutters up against the window, which had all this time remained shaded only by the curtains hastily drawn together on Esther's entrance, and the lighting of the candle.

She did all this with the same compressed lips, and the same stony look that her face had assumed on the first examination of the paper. Then she sat down for an instant to think; and, rising directly, went, with a step rendered firm by inward resolution of purpose, up the stairs; passed her own door, two steps, into her father's room. What did she want there?

I must tell you; I must put into words the dreadful secret which she believed that bit of paper had revealed to her.

Her father was the murderer!

That corner of stiff, shining, thick, writing paper, she recognised as a part of the sheet on which she had copied Samuel Bamford's beautiful lines so many months ago—copied (as you perhaps remember) on the blank part of a valentine sent to her by Jem Wilson, in those days when she did not treasure and hoard everything he had touched, as she would do now.

That copy had been given to her father for

whom it was made, and she had occasionally seen him reading it over, not a fortnight ago she was sure. But she resolved to ascertain if the other part still remained in his possession. He might,—it was just possible he *might*, have given it away to some friend; and if so, that person was the guilty one, for she could swear to the paper anywhere.

First of all she pulled out every article from the little old chest of drawers. Amongst them were some things which had belonged to her mother, but she had no time now to examine and try and remember them. All the reverence she could pay them was to carry them and lay them on the bed carefully, while the other things were tossed impatiently out upon the floor.

The copy of Bamford's lines was not there. Oh! perhaps he might have given it away; but then must it not have been to Jem? It was his gun.

And she set to with redoubled vigour to examine the deal box which served as chair, and which had once contained her father's Sunday clothes, in the days when he could afford to have Sunday clothes.

He had redeemed his better coat from the pawnshop before he left, that she had noticed. Here was his old one. What rustled under her hand in the pocket.

The paper! "Oh! Father!"

Yes, it fitted; jagged end to jagged end, letter to letter; and even the part which Esther had considered blank had its tallying mark with the larger piece, its tails of *ys* and *gs*. And then, as if that were not damning evidence enough, she felt again, and found some little bullets or shot (I don't know which you would call them) in that same pocket, along with a small paper parcel of gunpowder. As she was going to replace the jacket, having abstracted the paper, and bullets, etc., she saw a woollen gun-case, made of that sort of striped horse-cloth you must have seen a thousand times appropriated to such a purpose. The sight of it made her examine still further, but there was nothing else that could afford any evidence, so she locked the box, and sat down on the floor to contemplate the articles; now with a sickening despair, now with a kind of wondering curiosity, how her father had managed to evade observation. After all it was easy enough. He had evidently got possession of some gun (was it really Jem's? was he an accomplice? No! she did not believe it; he never, never would deliberately plan a murder with another, however he might be wrought up to it by passionate feeling at the time. Least of all would he accuse her to her father, without previously warning her; it was out of his nature).

Then having obtained possession of the gun, her father had loaded it at home, and might have carried it away with him some time when the neighbours were not noticing, and she was out, or asleep; and then he might have hidden it somewhere to be in readiness when he should want it. She was sure he had no such thing with him when he went away the last time.

She felt it was of no use to conjecture his motives. His actions had become so wild and irregular of late, that she could not reason upon them. Besides, was it not enough to know that he was guilty of this terrible offence? Her love for her father seemed to return with painful force, mixed up as it was with horror at his crime. That dear father who was once so kind, so warm-hearted, so ready to help either man or beast in distress, to murder! But in the desert of misery with which these thoughts surrounded her, the arid depths of whose gloom she dared not venture to contemplate, a little spring of comfort was gushing up at her feet, unnoticed at first, but soon to give her strength and hope.

And *that* was the necessity for exertion on her part which this discovery enforced.

Oh! I do think that the necessity for exertion, for some kind of action (bodily or mentally) in time of distress, is a most infinite blessing, although the first efforts at such seasons are painful. Something to be done implies that there is yet hope of some good thing to be accomplished, or some additional evil that may be avoided; and by degrees the hope absorbs much of the sorrow.

Emily Brontë

(1818–1848)

Born into a family of talented literary siblings, Emily Brontë spent most of her life in Yorkshire, England, which had been her home since the death of her mother in 1821. Emily, Charlotte, Anne, and their brother Branwell were raised by their aunt, Elizabeth Branwell. Emily went away to school in Cowan Bridge at the age of sixteen, but returned home in a year and worked briefly as a governess. On one of her few trips abroad, Emily studied languages with Charlotte in Brussels, but the wild Yorkshire moors she loved drew her back. When Aunt Branwell died, she never left home again.

Reserved and somewhat enigmatic, Emily frolicked only with her siblings, for the Brontës had collaborated on projects since childhood. She and Anne created an imaginary world called Gondal, and Emily wrote poems about it. Her first work appeared in the pseudonymous collection *Poems by Currer, Ellis and Acton Bell*, published in 1846 after Charlotte "discovered" Emily's (Ellis's) secret writings. Charlotte later wrote, "My sister Emily was not a person of demonstrative character, nor one, on the recesses of whose mind and feelings, even those nearest and dearest to her could, with impunity, intrude unlicensed; it took hours to reconcile her to the discovery I had made, and days to persuade her that such poems merited publication."

Though most of Emily Brontë's literary output was poetry, she is most famous for the dark romantic tragedy *Wuthering Heights* (1847). Recalling carefree days, before she realized that her beloved, Heathcliff, belonged to an inappropriate social class, the heroine Cathy swears, "I wish I were a girl again, half savage and hardy, and free." Brontë paints Heathcliff as brooding and lovelorn, but modern critics point out that today his behavior would be considered violent. The book is a complex, breathtaking saga of cruelty, cemeteries, ghosts, mysterious orphans, revenge, and as one contemporary reviewer has noted, an "aroma of incest" between Heathcliff and Catherine. Heathcliff, madly ardent but mildly sadistic, is described by Brontë as wolfish, a mad dog. Despite the allure of such emotional storytelling, *Wuthering Heights* was far from an immediate success. At the time of its publication, it was deemed morbid and unnecessarily dark of nature, "a disagreeable story."

Though Charlotte Brontë, who wrote *Jane Eyre*, has been called "the greatest female novelist of the post-Austen nineteenth century," Emily is now established as the family's finest poet. "Loud without the wind was roaring," she began one dramatically charged verse, reveling in her affinity with the uncontrollable forces of nature, as she had done when describing the windy moors where Heathcliff and Cathy roamed. It was a far greater affinity, apparently, than she ever had for people, for during her brief life, Emily Brontë never married, made few friends, and left little in the way of correspondence.

She died of consumption at the age of thirty, a year after the publication of *Wuthering Heights*. "I have never seen her parallel in anything," recalled Charlotte about Emily's deathbed demeanor, "stronger than a man, simpler than a child, her nature stood alone." As a tribute, Charlotte went on to revise the novel's errors and inconsistencies for the second edition, which appeared in 1850.

Retold through the voice of young Catherine Earnshaw's maid, Wuthering Heights *is a classic dramatic tale of doomed love between people of different social classes. Here, the observer eavesdrops on the impassioned reunion of Catherine and her maniacal lover, Heathcliff. Brontë also wrote poetry, as evidenced in the baleful lament "A.G.A."*

"Must I read it, ma'am? It is from Mr. Heathcliff."

There was a start and a troubled gleam of recollection, and a struggle to arrange her ideas. She lifted the letter, and seemed to peruse it; and when she came to the signature she sighed: yet still I found she had not gathered its import, for, upon my desiring to hear her reply, she merely pointed to the name, and gazed at me with mournful and questioning eagerness.

"Well, he wishes to see you," said I, guessing her need of an interpreter. "He's in the garden by this time, and impatient to know what answer I shall bring."

As I spoke, I observed a large dog lying on the sunny grass beneath raise its ears as if about to bark, and then smoothing them back, announce, by a wag of the tail, that someone approached whom it did not consider a stranger. Mrs. Linton bent forward, and listened breathlessly. The minute after a step traversed the hall; the open house was too tempting for Heathcliff to resist walking in: most likely he supposed that I was inclined to shirk my promise, and so resolved to trust to his own audacity. With straining eagerness Catherine gazed towards the entrance of her chamber. He did not hit the right room directly, she motioned me to admit him, but he

Emily Brontë

found it out ere I could reach the door, and in a stride or two was at her side, and had her grasped in his arms.

He neither spoke nor loosed his hold for some five minutes, during which period he bestowed more kisses than ever he gave in his life before, I dare say: but then my mistress had kissed him first, and I plainly saw that he could hardly bear, for downright agony, to look into her face! The same conviction had stricken him as me, from the instant he beheld her, that there was no prospect of ultimate recovery there—she was fated, sure to die.

"Oh, Cathy! Oh, my life! how can I bear it?" was the first sentence he uttered, in a tone that did not seek to disguise his despair. And now he stared at her so earnestly that I thought the very intensity of his gaze would bring tears into his eyes; but they burned with anguish: they did not melt.

"What now?" said Catherine, leaning back, and returning his look with a suddenly clouded brow: her humour was a mere vane for constantly varying caprices. "You and Edgar have broken my heart, Heathcliff! And you both came to bewail the deed to me, as if you were the people to be pitied! I shall not pity you, not I. You have killed me—and thriven on it, I think. How strong you are! How many years do you mean to live after I am gone?"

Heathcliff had knelt on one knee to embrace her; he attempted to rise, but she seized his hair, and kept him down.

"I wish I could hold you," she continued bitterly, "till we were both dead! I shouldn't care what you suffered. I care nothing for your sufferings. Why

shouldn't you suffer? I do! Will you forget me? Will you be happy when I am in the earth? Will you say twenty years hence, 'That's the grave of Catherine Earnshaw. I loved her long ago, and was wretched to lose her; but it is past. I've loved many others since: my children are dearer to me than she was; and at death, I shall not rejoice that I am going to her: I shall be sorry that I must leave them!' Will you say so, Heathcliff?"

"Don't torture me till I am as mad as yourself," cried he, wrenching his head free, and grinding his teeth.

The two, to a cool spectator, made a strange and fearful picture. Well might Catherine deem that heaven would be a land of exile to her, unless with her mortal body she cast away her moral character also. Her present countenance had a wild vindictiveness in its white cheek, and a bloodless lip and scintillating eye; and she retained in her closed fingers a portion of the locks she had been grasping. As to her companion, while raising himself with one hand, he had taken her arm with the other; and so inadequate was his stock of gentleness to the requirements of her condition, that on his letting go I saw four distinct impressions left blue in the colourless skin.

"Are you possessed with a devil," he pursued savagely, "to talk in that manner to me when you are dying? Do you reflect that all those words will be branded on my memory, and eating deeper eternally after you have left me? You know you lie to say I have killed you: and, Catherine, you know that I could as soon forget you as my existence! Is it not sufficient for your infernal selfishness, that while you are at peace I shall writhe in the torments of hell?"

"I shall not be at peace," moaned Catherine, recalled to a sense of physical weakness by the violent, unequal throbbing of her heart, which beat visibly and audibly under this excess of agitation. She said nothing further till the paroxysm was over; then she continued, more kindly—

"I'm not wishing you greater torment than I have, Heathcliff. I only wish us never to be parted: and should a word of mine distress you hereafter, think I feel the same distress underground, and for my own sake, forgive me! Come here and kneel down again! You never harmed me in your life. Nay, if you nurse anger, that will be worse to remember than my harsh words! Won't you come here again? Do!"

Heathcliff went to the back of her chair, and leant over, but not so far as to let her see his face, which was livid with emotion. She bent round to look at him; he would not permit it: turning abruptly, he walked to the fireplace, where he stood, silent, with his back towards us. Mrs. Linton's glance followed him suspiciously: every movement woke a new sentiment in her. After a pause and a prolonged gaze, she resumed; addressing me in accents of indignant disappointment—

"Oh, you see, Nelly, he would not relent a moment to keep me out of the grave. *That* is how I'm loved! Well, never mind. That is not *my* Heathcliff. I shall love mine yet; and take him with me: he's in my soul."

A.G.A.

Sleep brings no joy to me,
Remembrance never dies;
My soul is given to misery
And lives in sighs.

Sleep brings no rest to me;
The shadows of the dead
My waking eyes may never see
Surround my bed.

Sleep brings no hope to me;
In soundest sleep they come,
And with their doleful imagery
Deepen the gloom.

Sleep brings no strength to me,
No power renewed to brave:
I only sail a wilder sea,
A darker wave.

Sleep brings no friend to me
To soothe and aid to bear;
They all gaze, oh, how scornfully,
And I despair.

Sleep brings no wish to knit
My harassed heart beneath:
My only wish is to forget
In the sleep of death.

November 1837

George Eliot

George Eliot

(1819–1880)

"September 1856 made a new era in my life, for it was then I began to write fiction," wrote Mary Ann Evans, who took a masculine pen name so that she might be taken more seriously. She has come to be known as one of the greatest British novelists, praised for her wise observations on life and society.

At the age of thirteen, Eliot attended school in Coventry, near the Staffordshire village where she was born. An exemplary student, she studied foreign languages, philosophy, theology, and literature. Her first work, published in the *Westminster Review*, was a collection of comic stories called "Silly Novels by Lady Novelist," in which she dismissed the popular religious literature of the time as fodder for the brainless. In her early twenties, she made the acquaintance of Charles Bray, a Coventry manufacturer who espoused the radical, free-thinking rhetoric of the day—an intriguing concept for the philosophically minded Eliot. For many years, she corresponded with Harriet Beecher Stowe, the American author of the best-selling *Uncle Tom's Cabin*, about how best to integrate writing into a domestic life.

Though she didn't marry until the age of 60, men exerted powerful influences over Eliot's life. In 1850, while working as an editor at the *Westminster Review*, Eliot fell in love with publisher John Chapman. Her passion was unrequited, despite the fact that Eliot lived for a time in Chapman's home. She befriended Ivan Turgenev, the Russian novelist and playwright, and explored Positivism, the psychological, self-revelatory fashion of the day. Her most significant relationship, begun in 1854, was with George Henry Lewes, a philsospher and writer. Though religious beliefs prevented him from divorcing, he and Eliot lived together for the rest of his life.

Lewes urged her to hone her writing skills by reading the works of Jane Austen. One spring day, on holiday on the island of Jersey, she read the entire novel *Emma* aloud to him. Eliot in turn helped Lewes with his research, and after his death completed his important work on psychology, *Problems of Life and Mind.*

The worlds she created in *Adam Bede* (1859), *The Mill on the Floss* (1860), *Silas Marner* (1861), and other works were imperfect ones. Adultery was a common theme, and her female characters tended to be foolish if admirable souls. Virginia Woolf called Eliot's *Middlemarch* (1872) "one of the few English novels written for grown-up people." Its heroine, Dorothea Brooke, was inspired by the life of Saint Theresa of Avila. *Daniel Deronda* (published serially, 1874-76 was Eliot's last novel. By then she had imbued her women with more righteous aggression: the protagonist pushes her abusive husband off a sailboat.

Three years after Lewes died, Eliot wed her financial advisor, John Walter Cross, twenty years her junior. She died seven months later, recognized by many as the greatest English novelist of her time.

Maggie Tulliver is the free-spirited heroine of The Mill on the Floss, *George Eliot's insightful study of life in a rural English village, whose denizens Maggie finds gossipy and class-conscious. Though they often quarrel, Maggie adores her brother Tom, and fears for his safety when flood waters threaten.*

At that moment Maggie felt a startling sensation of sudden cold about her knees and feet: it was water flowing under her. She started up—the stream was flowing under the door that led into the passage. She was not bewildered for an instant—she knew it was the flood!

The tumult of emotion she had been enduring for the last twelve hours seemed to have left a great calm in her: without screaming, she hurried with the candle upstairs to Bob Jakin's bedroom. The door was ajar—she went in and shook him by the shoulder.

"Bob, the Flood is come! it is in the house! let us see if we can make the boats safe."

She lighted his candle, while the poor wife, snatching up her baby, burst into screams; and then she hurried down again to see if the waters were rising fast. There was a step down into the room at the door leading from the staircase: she saw that the water was already on the level with the step. While she was looking, something came with a tremendous crash against the window, and sent the leaded panes and the old wooden framework inwards in shivers,— the water pouring in after it.

"It is the boat!" cried Maggie. "Bob, come down to get the boats!"

And without a moment's shudder of fear, she plunged through the water, which was rising fast to her knees, and by the glimmering light of the candle she had left on the stairs, she mounted on to the window-sill, and crept into the boat, which was left with the prow lodging and protruding through the window. Bob was not long after her, hurrying without shoes or stockings, but with the lanthorn in his hand.

"Why, they're both here—both the boats," said Bob, as he got into the one where Maggie was. "It's wonderful this fastening isn't broke too, as well as the mooring."

In the excitement of getting into the other boat, unfastening it and mastering an oar, Bob was not struck with the danger Maggie incurred. We are not apt to fear for the fearless, when we are companions in their danger, and Bob's mind was absorbed in possible expedients for the safety of the helpless indoors. The fact that Maggie had been up, had waked him, and had taken the lead in activity, gave Bob a vague impression of her as one who would help to protect, not need to be protected. She too had got possession of an oar, and had pushed off, so as to release the boat from the overhanging window-frame.

"The water's rising so fast," said Bob, "I doubt it'll be in at the chambers before long—th' house is so low. I've more mind to get Prissy and the child and the mother into the boat, if I could and trusten to the water—for th' old house is none so safe. And if I let go the boat—but *you*," he exclaimed, suddenly lifting the light of his lanthorn on Maggie, as she stood in the rain with the oar in her hand and her black hair streaming.

Maggie had no time to answer, for a new tidal current swept along the line of the houses, and drove both the boats out on to the wide water, with a force that carried them far past the meeting current of the river.

In the first moments Maggie felt nothing, thought of nothing, but that she had suddenly passed away from that life which she had been dreading: it was the transition of death, without its agony—and she was alone in the darkness with God.

The whole thing had been so rapid—so dreamlike—that the threads of ordinary association were broken: she sank down on the seat clutching the oar mechanically, and for a long while had no distinct conception of her position. The first thing that waked her to fuller consciousness, was the cessation of the rain, and a perception that the darkness was divided by the faintest light, which parted the overhanging gloom from the immeasurable watery level below. She was driven out upon the flood:—that awful visitation of God which her father used to talk of—which had made the nightmare of her childish dreams. And with that thought there rushed in the vision of the old home—and Tom—and her mother—they had all listened together.

"O God, where am I? Which is the way home?" she cried out, in the dim loneliness.

What was happening to them at the Mill? The flood had once nearly destroyed it. They might be in danger—in distress: her mother and her brother, alone there, beyond reach of help! Her whole soul was strained now on that thought; and she saw the long-loved faces looking for help into the darkness, and finding none.

She was floating in smooth water now—perhaps far on the over-flooded fields. There was no sense of present danger to check the outgoing of her mind to the old home; and she strained her eyes against the curtain of gloom that she might seize the first sight of her whereabout—that she might catch some faint suggestion of the spot towards which all her anxieties tended.

O how welcome, the widening of that dismal watery level—the gradual uplifting of the cloudy firmament—the slowly defining blackness of objects above the glassy dark! Yes—she must be out on the fields—those were the tops of hedgerow trees. Which way did the river lie? Looking behind her, she saw the lines of black trees: looking before her there were none: then, the river lay before her. She seized an oar and began to paddle the boat forward with the energy of wakening hope: the dawning seemed to advance more swiftly, now she was in action; and she could soon see the poor dumb beasts crowding piteously on a mound where they had taken refuge. Onward she paddled and rowed by turns in the grow-

ing twilight: her wet clothes clung round her, and her streaming hair was dashed about by the wind, but she was hardly conscious of any bodily sensations—except a sensation of strength, inspired by mighty emotion. Along with the sense of danger and possible rescue for those long-remembered beings at the old home, there was an undefined sense of reconcilement with her brother: what quarrel, what harshness, what unbelief in each other can subsist in the presence of a great calamity when all the artificial vesture of our life is gone, and we are all one with each other in primitive mortal needs? Vaguely, Maggie felt this;—in the strong resurgent love towards her brother that swept away all the later impressions of hard, cruel offence and misunderstanding, and left only the deep, underlying, unshakable memories of early union.

Emily Dickinson

(1830–1886)

"I'm nobody. Who are you?" asked the poet Emily Elizabeth Dickinson, scrawling the words in her large, swirling handwriting, punctuated with bold dashes of the pen. In the eyes of scholars, eccentric Emily was far from nobody, but the question of exactly what circumstances in her personal life inspired the withdrawn, unmarried "belle of Amherst" to write with such passion is one which has intrigued her devotees for decades.

Some details of Dickinson's life are known. She was born in Amherst, Massachusetts, to a family zealous about education and politics. Her father was a prominent lawyer. Dickinson was a voracious reader—she adored Elizabeth Barrett Browning, as well as Emerson, though her primary focus was on women's literature. After attending Amherst Academy between 1834 and 1847, she spent a year at Mount Holyoke College.

Dickinson began writing poetry as an adolescent. Her period of greatest creativity began in her early thirties, when she generated poems by the hundreds. Witty and outgoing as a girl, Dickinson grew shy in later life, and by her forties, simply refused to leave the house. In 1861, she was devastated by the death of her role model, Elizabeth Barrett Browning. About Browning she wrote, "Her—'last Poems'—Poets—ended—Silver—perished—with her Tongue—Not on Record—bubbled other, Flute—or Woman—so divine."

Dickinson is often referred to as a "metaphysical poet" for the way in which she linked her seemingly coy, girlish sentiments with a profound spiritualism. Because her poems were so unusual in their form and content, she was initially regarded as a minor poet. Now, of course, she is appreciated as a major writer of awesome originality. Recurrent themes in her work include the natural world and writing as an almost religious vocation. Dickinson had a maudlin side and often wrote of death, shipwrecks, storms, volcanoes, funerals, and prisons.

In one of her best-known poems, "Because I could not stop for Death," death takes the form of a gentle-man caller.

Speculating about the possibility of Dickinson's secret love life has long provided sport for literary scholars. While she avoided strangers, the poet did maintain a number of intimate correspondences—some with people she had never met, whose work she admired, as they did hers. One of her confidantes, Charles Wadsworth, was a minister. Another, Samuel Bowles, was an editor. Both are rumored to have been Dickinson's lovers, and one or the other may have broken her heart.

Emily died at age fifty-six. Only seven of her creations were published during her lifetime—and those appeared without attribution, and heavily edited. Searching through Emily's effects, her sister Lavinia discovered hundreds of hidden poems, some of which Emily had copied into packets meticulously sewn together, and others scribbled in the blank spaces of candy wrappers, shopping lists, and envelopes. An edited, partial edition of the poems was published in 1890, to a warm critical and popular reception. A complete scholarly edition of 1,775 poems, astonishing in its breadth, was finally compiled in 1955. At last, Dickinson received the full attention her work deserved.

There is a certain apprehensive quality to Emily Dickinson's poems, a nervous, intelligent energy that owes as much to the verses' unusual structure as to the insight of their messages. These two, among her best known, were published after her death. Dickinson did not assign titles to most of her poems, and they are referred to by their first lines.

There's a certain Slant of light,
Winter Afternoons—
That oppresses, like the Heft
Of Cathedral Tunes—

Heavenly Hurt, it gives us—
We can find no scar,
But internal difference,
Where the Meanings, are—

None may teach it—Any—
'Tis the Seal Despair—
An imperial affliction
Sent us of the Air—

When it comes, the Landscape listens—
Shadows—hold their breath—
When it goes, 'tis like the Distance
On the look of Death—

circa 1861

Emily Dickinson

Because I could not stop for Death—
He kindly stopped for me—
The Carriage held but just Ourselves—
And Immortality.

We slowly drove—He knew no haste
And I had put away
My labor and my leisure too,
For His Civility—

We passed the School, where Children strove
At Recess—in the Ring—
We passed the Fields of Gazing Grain—
We passed the Setting Sun—

Or rather—He passed Us—
The Dews drew quivering and chill—
For only Gossamer, my Gown—
My Tippet—only Tulle—

We paused before a House that seemed
A Swelling of the Ground—
The Roof was scarcely visible—
The Cornice—in the Ground—

Since then—'tis Centuries—and yet
Feels shorter than the Day
I first surmised the Horses' Heads
Were toward Eternity—

circa 1863

Sarah Orne Jewett

(1849–1909)

The daughter of a doctor specializing in "obstetrics and diseases of women and children," Theodora Sarah Orne Jewett so admired her father's profession that she longed to become a physician herself. Ironically, illness prevented her from pursuing medicine as a career. Instead she devoted herself to writing, living most of her days in the Maine coastal village of South Berwick, where she had been born in 1849. Jewett sold her first story, a lovingly rendered vignette of everyday life in Maine, when she was eighteen. It was the beginning of a career writing "local color" pieces, which she sold to *Harper's*, *The Century*, and *The Atlantic*. Her first collection of sketches, *Deephaven*, was published in 1877. She subsequently authored several volumes of poetry and fourteen short-story collections.

Many of Jewett's works feature strong bonds of friendship between women. Her own relationship with Annie Fields, wife of *The Atlantic* magazine publisher James T. Fields, was described by observers as a model of what was called the "Boston marriage," a long-term, monogamous relationship between two otherwise unmarried women. The two socialized with a circle of other single women friends, all involved in creative endeavors—poets, writers, musicians, artists. Jewett never married, but she was fond of children and published a number of stories for younger readers.

To marry or not to marry: that is the choice faced by the character Nan Leslie in *A Country Doctor* (1884), Jewett's vaguely autobiographical tale of a woman forced to choose between marriage to an attractive young bachelor or an independent career as a country doctor in Maine. Its feminist edge is palpable, as is Jewett's portrayal of the tension between city and country life, and the difficult decision of whether to work and be productive, or to lounge in the lap of married luxury.

Jewett loved the country. In her most famous book, *The Country of the Pointed Firs* (1896), she recounts details of the pastoral world in which she lived: "On the coast of Maine, where many green islands and salt inlets fringe the deep-cut shore line; where balsam firs and bayberry bushes send their fragrance far seaward, and song-sparrows sing all day. . ." Despite the rich texture of her writing, Jewett's work was largely neglected until women's studies scholars revived it, for critics of the time found her vision too limited and her narratives too sketchy. It took a colleague, the writer Willa Cather, to dub *The Country of the Pointed Firs* an American classic in the vein of Hawthorne and Twain. Cather pointed out that at the time Jewett was writing, stories about New England were popular, and those in the mainstream may have appealed more to readers because of their adventure-filled plots. Still, she noted, such stories lack what Jewett's offer: "inherent, individual beauty; the kind of beauty we feel when a beautiful song is sung by a beautiful voice that is exactly suited to the song." Jewett continued to write until she suffered a crippling accident in 1902. She died seven years later.

Set in a Maine seaport before the turn of the century, The Country of the Pointed Firs *is related by a narrator who observes the tangled relationships and petty verities of this small-town life in rich detail. Here the narrator, who is just visiting, meets one of the town's most interesting characters.*

At first the tiny house of Mrs. Almira Todd, which stood with its end to the street, appeared to be retired and sheltered enough from the busy world, behind its bushy bit of a green garden, in which all the blooming things, two or three gay hollyhocks and some London-pride, were pushed back against the gray-shingled wall. It was a queer little garden and puzzling to a stranger, the few flowers being put at a disadvantage by so much greenery; but the discovery was soon made that Mrs. Todd was an ardent lover of herbs, both wild and tame, and the sea-breezes blew into the low end-window of the house laden with not only sweet-brier and sweet-mary, but balm and sage and borage and mint, wormwood and southern-wood. If Mrs. Todd had occasion to step into the far corner of her herb plot, she trod heavily upon thyme, and made its fragrant presence known with all the rest. Being a very large person, her full skirts brushed and bent almost every slender stalk that her feet missed. You could always tell when she was stepping about there, even when you were half awake in the morning, and learned to know, in the course of a few weeks' experience, in exactly which corner of the garden she might be.

At one side of this herb plot were other growths of a rustic pharmocopœia, great treasures and rarities among the commoner herbs. There were some strange and pungent odors that roused a dim sense and remembrance of something in the forgotten past. Some of these might once have belonged to sacred and mystic rites, and have had some occult knowledge handed with them down the centuries; but

Sarah Orne Jewett

now they pertained only to humble compounds brewed at intervals with molasses or vinegar or spirits in a small caldron on Mrs. Todd's kitchen stove. They were dispensed to suffering neighbors, who usually came at night as if by stealth, bringing their own ancient-looking vials to be filled. One nostrum was called the Indian remedy, and its price was but fifteen cents; the whispered directions could be heard as customers passed the windows. With most remedies the purchaser was allowed to depart unadmonished from the kitchen, Mrs. Todd being a wise saver of steps; but with certain vials she gave cautions, standing in the doorway, and there were other doses which had to be accompanied on their healing way as far as the gate, while she muttered long chapters of directions, and kept up an air of secrecy and importance to the last. It may not have been only the common ails of humanity with which she tried to cope; it seemed sometimes as if love and hate and jealousy and adverse winds at sea might also find their proper remedies among the curious wild-looking plants in Mrs. Todd's garden.

The village doctor and this learned herbalist were upon the best of terms. The good man may have counted upon the unfavorable effect of certain potions which he should find his opportunity in counteracting; at any rate, he now and then stopped and exchanged greetings with Mrs. Todd over the picket fence. The conversation became at once professional after the briefest preliminaries, and he would stand twirling a sweet-scented sprig in his fingers, and make suggestive jokes, perhaps about her

faith in a too persistent course of thoroughwort elixir, in which my landlady professed such firm belief as sometimes to endanger the life and usefulness of worthy neighbors.

To arrive at this quietest of seaside villages late in June, when the busy herb-gathering season was just beginning, was also to arrive in the early prime of Mrs. Todd's activity in the brewing of old-fashioned spruce beer. This cooling and refreshing drink had been brought to wonderful perfection through a long series of experiments; it had won immense local fame, and the supplies for its manufacture were always giving out and having to be replenished. For various reasons, the seclusion and uninterrupted days which had been looked forward to proved to be very rare in this otherwise delightful corner of the world. My hostess and I had made our shrewd business agreement on the basis of a simple cold luncheon at noon, and liberal restitution in the matter of hot suppers, to provide for which the lodger might sometimes be seen hurrying down the road, late in the day, with cunner line in hand. It was soon found that this arrangement made large allowance for Mrs. Todd's slow herb-gathering progresses through woods and pastures. The spruce-beer customers were pretty steady in hot weather, and there were many demands for different soothing syrups and elixirs with which the unwise curiosity of my early residence had made me acquainted. Knowing Mrs. Todd to be a widow, who had little beside this slender business and the income from one hungry lodger to maintain her, one's energies and even interest were quickly bestowed, until it became a matter of course that she should go afield every pleasant day, and that the lodger should answer all peremptory knocks at the side door.

In taking an occasional wisdom-giving stroll in Mrs. Todd's company, and in acting as business partner during her frequent absences, I found the July days fly fast, and it was not until I felt myself confronted with too great pride and pleasure in the display, one night, of two dollars and twenty-seven cents which I had taken in during the day, that I remembered a long piece of writing, sadly belated now, which I was bound to do. To have been patted kindly on the shoulder and called "darlin'," to have been offered a surprise of early mushrooms for supper, to have had all the glory of making two dollars and twenty-seven cents in a single day, and then to renounce it all and withdraw from these pleasant successes, needed much resolution. Literary employ-ments are so vexed with uncertainties at best, and it was not until the voice of conscience sounded louder in my ears than the sea on the nearest pebble beach that I said unkind words of withdrawal to Mrs. Todd. She only became more wistfully affectionate than ever in her expressions, and looked as disappointed as I expected when I frankly told her that I could no longer enjoy the pleasure of what we called "seein' folks." I felt that I was cruel to a whole neighborhood in curtailing her liberty in this most important season for harvesting the different wild herbs that were so much counted upon to ease their winter ails.

"Well, dear," she said sorrowfully, "I've took great advantage o' your bein' here. I ain't had such a season for years, but I have never had nobody I could so trust. All you lack is a few qualities, but with time you'd gain judgment an' experience, an' be very able in the business. I'd stand right here an' say it to anybody."

Kate Chopin

(1851–1904)

The death of her husband Oscar was the catalyst of Kate Chopin's plunge into the literary world. Left with six children to support, she began writing stories for the leading popular magazines of the day. Soon, her work was making waves for its unorthodox portrayals of women and marriage.

Chopin was born Kate O'Flaherty in St. Louis, Missouri. Her father was a well-to-do Irish merchant and a devoted parent; he died in a dramatic train wreck when Kate was four. At age seventeen, Kate graduated from a local private school. A year later, she met her husband, Oscar Chopin, who had left his native New Orleans to pursue a banking career in St. Louis. They married and moved to New Orleans, where her own maternal ancestors, Creoles who emigrated from France, had also settled. Chopin spent a decade in that city, bearing and caring for children. When Oscar's business failed, the family moved to a small Louisiana village. This gave Chopin the opportunity to observe the rural Acadian, or Cajun, culture, which was to appear in many of her writings later on—particularly the early ones in which she relied heavily on vignettes of local color.

Not long after Oscar's death from swamp fever in 1882, Chopin returned to St. Louis. In 1887, she began writing at the urging of her family physician, a friend who had been impressed by the narrative quality of her letters to him. By 1890, prestigious literary magazines had published a number of her short stories set in the bayou region of Louisiana where she had once lived; they were later collected in *Bayou Folk* (1894). The same year, Chopin's first novel, *At Fault*, was published. This sympathetic look at divorce, a taboo subject at the time, brought her notoriety for her untraditional view of women's place in marriage, and her skepticism about marital bonds.

Kate Chopin

Chopin's fictional departures from conventional morality continued in her second story collection, *A Night in Acadie* (1897). Its heroines were aggressive, passionate women who willingly indulged in pleasures of both body ("When he touched her breasts they gave themselves up in quivering ecstacy, inviting his lips") and self (a character in "A Pair of Silk Stockings" finds $15 and treats herself to new hose, shoes, gloves, magazines, a fine meal and a matinee, all in one afternoon).

These gradual literary indiscretions led to the creation of Chopin's best and most famous novel, *The Awakening* (1899). Though it seems a benign enough tale, the book created a furor. *The Awakening* relates the story of Edna Pontellier, a wife and devoted mother who fantasizes about having an affair with a younger man, and explores the consequences of women's emotional restlessness in a stirring way. The tale ends in tragedy when Edna, who has learned to swim in this summer of her awakening, surrenders herself to the freedom of the open sea. The book was banned by bookstores and libraries during Chopin's lifetime, and languished in ignominy after her death in 1904. In the 1960s it was rediscovered by women's literature scholars and is now considered a classic.

In The Awakening, *Chopin captures the lazy rhythms of wealthy Creoles vacationing at the seaside. She also explores the growing frustration of a woman who feels trapped in a loveless marriage and aroused by the off-handed attentions of a young man on holiday at the same resort community.*

Edna had attempted all summer to learn to swim. She had received instructions from both the men and women; in some instances from the children. Robert had pursued a system of lessons almost daily; and he was nearly at the point of discouragement in realizing the futility of his efforts. A certain ungovernable dread hung about her when in the water, unless there was a hand near by that might reach out and reassure her.

But that night she was like the little tottering, stumbling, clutching child, who of a sudden realizes its powers, and walks for the first time alone, boldly and with over-confidence. She could have shouted for joy. She did shout for joy, as with a sweeping stroke or two she lifted her body to the surface of the water.

A feeling of exultation overtook her, as if some power of significant import had been given her to control the working of her body and her soul. She grew daring and reckless, overestimating her strength. She wanted to swim far out, where no woman had swum before.

Her unlooked-for achievement was the subject of wonder, applause, and admiration. Each one congratulated himself that his special teachings had accomplished this desired end.

"How easy it is!" she thought. "It is nothing," she said aloud; "why did I not discover before that it was nothing? Think of the time I have lost splashing about like a baby!" She would not join the groups in their sports and bouts, but intoxicated with her newly conquered power, she swam out alone.

She turned her face seaward to gather in an impression of space and solitude, which the vast expanse of water, meeting and melting with the moonlit sky, conveyed to her excited fancy. As she swam, she seemed to be reaching out for the unlimited in which to lose herself.

Once she turned and looked toward the shore, toward the people she had left there. She had not gone any great distance—that is, what would have been a great distance for an experienced swimmer. But to her unaccustomed vision the stretch of water behind her assumed the aspect of a barrier which her unaided strength would never be able to overcome.

A quick vision of death smote her soul, and for a second of time appalled and enfeebled her senses. But by an effort she rallied her staggering faculties and managed to regain the land.

She made no mention of her encounter with death and her flash of terror, except to say to her husband, "I thought I should have perished out there alone."

"You were not so very far, my dear; I was watching you," he told her.

Edna went at once to the bath-house, and she had put on her dry clothes and was ready to return home before the others had left the water. She started to walk away alone. They all called to her and shouted to her. She waved a dissenting hand, and went on, paying no further heed to their renewed cries which sought to detain her.

"Sometimes I am tempted to think that

Mrs. Pontellier is capricious," said Madame Lebrun, who was amusing herself immensely and feared that Edna's abrupt departure might put an end to the pleasure.

"I know she is," assented Mr. Pontellier; "sometimes, not often."

Edna had not traversed a quarter of the distance on her way home before she was overtaken by Robert.

"Did you think I was afraid?" she asked him, without a shade of annoyance.

"No; I knew you weren't afraid."

"Then why did you come? Why didn't you stay out there with the others?"

"I never thought of it."

"Thought of what?"

"Of anything. What difference does it make?"

"I'm very tired," she uttered, complainingly.

"I know you are."

"You don't know anything about it. Why should you know? I never was so exhausted in my life. But it isn't unpleasant. A thousand emotions have swept through me tonight. I don't comprehend half of them. Don't mind what I'm saying; I am just thinking aloud. I wonder if I shall ever be stirred again as Mademoiselle Reisz's playing moved me tonight. I wonder if any night on earth will ever again be like this one. It is like a night in a dream. The people about me are like some uncanny, half-human beings. There must be spirits abroad to-night."

"There are," whispered Robert. "Didn't you know this was the twenty-eighth of August?"

"The twenty-eighth of August?"

"Yes. On the twenty-eighth of August, at the hour of midnight, and if the moon is shining—the moon must be shining—a spirit that has haunted these shores for ages rises up from the Gulf. With its own penetrating vision the spirit seeks some one mortal worthy to hold him company, worthy of being exalted for a few hours into realms of the semi-celestials. His search has always hitherto been fruitless, and he has sunk back, disheartened, into the sea. But to-night he found Mrs. Pontellier. Perhaps he will never wholly release her from the spell. Perhaps she will never again suffer a poor, unworthy earthling to walk in the shadow of her divine presence."

"Don't banter me," she said, wounded at what appeared to be his flippancy. He did not mind the entreaty; but the tone with its delicate note of pathos was like a reproach. He could not explain; he could not tell her that he had penetrated her mood and understood. He said nothing except to offer her his arm, for, by her own admission, she was exhausted. She had been walking alone with her arms hanging limp, letting her white skirts trail along the dewy path. She took his arm, but she did not lean upon it. She let her hand lie listlessly, as though her thoughts were elsewhere—somewhere in advance of her body, and she was striving to overtake them.

Edith Wharton

(1862–1937)

Edith Newbold Jones was born into a silver-spoon life of privilege. Her parents, Lucretia Rhinelander Jones and George Jones, were New York City patricians whose ancestors had attended the Boston Tea Party. The youngest of three children, Edith began making up stories as a toddler, and at age sixteen, was the proud author of a vanity-press volume of poetry called *Verses*.

In 1885 she married Edward Wharton, a courtly older gentleman known as Teddy. This ensured her a place in the "right" society, but Wharton was dissatisfied. Depressed by the restrictions of marriage and upper-class life, she began writing about what she had observed in the glittering drawing-rooms of wealthy Manhattan: the idle but charged cocktail-party chatter, and the desperate emotions seething beneath high society's starched collars. Thanks to the freedom afforded by her wealth, Wharton was able to roam the world. She began writing travelogues, in addition to articles for *Scribner's* and *Harper's*, and stories that found their way into novels. On some of these trips, she also underwent treatment for nervous disorder. After twenty-eight years of marriage spent in Paris, New York, and New England, the Whartons divorced, and Edith fled to Paris. There she met the distinguished American novelist Henry James, who became a close friend and colleague.

The House of Mirth (1905) first established Wharton as a major literary force. Its subject was the fashionable New York milieu she knew so well. Critical of that shallow world's power over both people and their values, the book is a highly dramatic, elegantly written satire, a raging bonfire of vanities in the mannerly tradition of Jane Austen. *Ethan Frome* (1911) is a simple tale about a man haunted by unrequited passion for the cousin of his ailing wife, and his longing to break with convention. By the time *The Custom of the Country* (1913) was

Edith Wharton

published—another scathing, albeit ladylike, indictment of current morals—Wharton had become a commercially successful author.

When World War I broke out in 1914, Wharton volunteered in the relief effort in France, for which she was awarded the Cross of the Legion of Honor. Her controversial novel *Summer* (1918) was praised by Joseph Conrad, an admirer of Wharton's. This frank exploration of a mature woman's sensual awakening was considered explicitly sexual for the times, and was inspired by her great love affair with the worldly Morton Fullerton, a friend of Henry James. Their romance began in 1907 when Wharton was forty-five, and lasted for three years. It is said that she wanted to marry, and he wished to remain single.

Wharton's greatest achievement was winning the Pulitzer Prize with the 1920 publication of *The Age of Innocence*, another sendup of hypocritical society, leavened with a stirring dose of unrequited love. "There it was before me," she went on to write about that world in *A Backward Glance* (1934), her autobiography, "in all its flatness and futility, asking to be dealt with as the theme most available to my hand, since I had been steeped in it from infancy." The 1990s have seen a revival of interest in Wharton's work with both *The Age of Innocence* and *Ethan Frome* filmed for the big screen. Regarded in her own lifetime as a leading American author, Wharton died in her garden in the South of France.

Reading the short novel **Summer** *(1918) is as relaxing as sitting by the sea. In this selection, the protagonist, a young woman of poor means named Charity Royall, hides in the dark and peers through his window into the bedroom of Lucas Harney, the man she loves. Charity believes he will help her escape the inevitable hardships of her life. Oh, if she only knew!*

Harney was still unaware of her presence. He sat without moving, moodily staring before him at the same spot in the wall-paper. He had not even had the energy to finish his packing, and his clothes and papers lay on the floor about the portmanteau. Presently he unlocked his clasped hands and stood up; and Charity, drawing back hastily, sank down on the step of the verandah. The night was so dark that there was not much chance of his seeing her unless he opened the window, and before that she would have time to slip away and be lost in the shadow of the trees. He stood for a minute or two looking around the room with the same expression of self-disgust, as if he hated himself and everything about him; then he sat down again at the table, drew a few more strokes, and threw his pencil aside. Finally he walked across the floor, kicking the portmanteau out of his way, and lay down on the bed, folding his arms under his head, and staring up morosely at the ceiling. Just so, Charity had seen him at her side, on the grass or the pine-needles, his eyes fixed on the sky, and pleasure flashing over his face like the flickers of sun the branches shed on it. But now the face was so changed that she hardly knew it; and grief at his grief gathered in her throat, rose to her eyes and ran over.

She continued to crouch on the steps, holding her breath and stiffening herself into complete immobility. One motion of her hand, one tap on the pane, and she could picture the sudden change in his face. In every pulse of her rigid body she was aware of the welcome his eyes and lips would give her; but something kept her from moving. It was not the fear of any sanction, human or heavenly; she had never in her life been afraid. It was simply that she had suddenly understood what would happen if she went in. It was the thing that *did* happen between young men and girls, and that North Dormer ignored in public and snickered over on the sly. It was what Miss Hatchard was still ignorant of, but every girl of Charity's class knew about before she left school. It was what had happened to Ally Hawes's sister Julia, and had ended in her going to Nettleton, and in people's never mentioning her name.

It did not, of course, always end so sensationally; nor, perhaps, on the whole, so untragically. Charity had always suspected that the shunned Julia's fate might have its compensations. There were other worse endings that the village knew of, mean, miserable, unconfessed; other lives that went on drearily, without visible change, in the same cramped setting of hypocrisy. But these were not the reasons that held her back. Since the day before, she had known exactly what she would feel if Harney should take her in his arms: the melting of palm into palm and mouth on mouth, and the long flame burning her from head to foot. But mixed with this feeling was another: the wondering pride in his liking for her, the startled soft-

ness that his sympathy had put into her heart. Sometimes, when her youth flushed up in her, she had imagined yielding like other girls to furtive caresses in the twilight; but she could not so cheapen herself to Harney. She did not know why he was going; but since he was going she felt she must do nothing to deface the image of her that he carried away. If he wanted her he must seek her: he must not be surprised into taking her as girls like Julia Hawes were taken. . . .

No sound came from the sleeping village, and in the deep darkness of the garden she heard now and then a secret rustle of branches, as though some night-bird brushed them. Once a footfall passed the gate, and she shrank back into her corner; but the steps died away and left a profounder quiet. Her eyes were still on Harney's tormented face: she felt she could not move till he moved. But she was beginning to grow numb from her constrained position, and at times her thoughts were so indistinct that she seemed to be held there only by a vague weight of weariness.

A long time passed in this strange vigil. Harney still lay on the bed, motionless and with fixed eyes, as though following his vision to its bitter end. At last he stirred and changed his attitude slightly, and Charity's heart began to tremble. But he only flung out his arms and sank back into his former position. With a deep sigh he tossed the hair from his forehead; then his whole body relaxed, his head turned sideways on the pillow, and she saw that he had fallen asleep. The sweet expression came back to his lips, and the haggardness faded from his face, leaving it as fresh as a boy's.

She rose and crept away.

Willa Cather

(1876–1947)

Mother Earth, crowned with fields of wheat, corn and prairie grass, is the most compelling character in the stories of Willa Sibert Cather. She is best known for chronicling the lives of brave settlers—primarily women—who traveled America's western frontier in the mid-to-late nineteenth century. Cather was familiar with the territory, having moved from her birthplace near Winchester, Virginia, to the big-sky country of Red Cloud, Nebraska, at the age of eight. In 1895, she graduated from the state university there.

Cather taught journalism and literature in Pittsburgh, writing poetry and short stories in her free time. This taste of the literary life prompted her to move to New York City, where she found work as an editor at *McClure's Magazine*. It was there, too, that she met Edith Lewis, the woman who became her lifetime companion. Sarah Orne Jewett, a contemporary writer and, like Cather, an astute observer of the natural world, became her literary mentor.

In *O Pioneers!* (1913), her second novel, Cather introduces the Swedish immigrant family of Alexandra Bergson, a strong-willed woman who takes over her father's role, running a huge farm on the prairie. Bergson, who fears romantic passion will diminish her power to control the business, chooses to express herself in such solitary pursuits as canning fruit and working the land. Critics praised Cather's descriptions of the Midwestern landscape, calling them unusual for a woman schooled in the journalistic traditions of a man's world.

Cather loved the opera and knew many of its singers. In *The Song of the Lark* (1915), she depicts the harrowing physical labor required for opera performances. "If you love the good thing vitally, enough to give up for it all that one must give up, then you must hate the cheap thing just as hard. I tell you there is such a thing as creative hate!" swears its ambitious heroine, Thea Kronberg. Using voluptuous female imagery, Cather implies that the untamed canyonland of the Southwest is a more appropriate place for an independent woman that the dainty, manicured gardens of Kronberg's own "civilized" world. Though *The Song of the Lark* received critical acclaim, Cather was unhappy with it and actually disavowed it upon its 1932 republication.

       Stubborn-minded and physically formidable, the Bohemian immigrant Antonia Shimerda of *My Antonia* (1918) is Cather's most compelling heroine. Like Alexandra Bergson, Antonia's grand passion is her family's Midwestern farm. Some scholars consider *A Lost Lady* (1923), an Electra story in which the mother-figure meets a tragic end, to be Cather's masterpiece. *One of Ours* (1923), about a Nebraska farm boy who dies on the Western Front of World War I, won a Pulitzer Prize in 1924. Cather went on to write *The Professor's House* (1925), a tale of a distinguished, middle-aged professor's retreat from life, and *Death Comes to the Archbishop* (1927), about a French priest's missionary work in New Mexico. Though her literary vision gradually widened, Cather's later novels bespeak a familiar spiritual attachment to the wide-open spaces of the American West.

A magnificent yet simply told portrait of Antonia Shimerda, a hardy Czech girl who works her family's farm in the Midwest, My Antonia *is Cather's masterpiece. This excerpt—in the voice of the book's narrator, Jim, who lives on a neighboring farm—captures the vigor of life among Bohemian immigrant farmers in the early part of the twentieth century.*

When the sun was dropping low, Antonia came up the big south draw with her team. How much older she had grown in eight months! She had come to us a child, and now she was a tall, strong young girl, although her fifteenth birthday had just slipped by. I ran out and met her as she brought her horses up to the windmill to water them. She wore the boots her father had so thoughtfully taken off before he shot himself, and his old fur cap. Her outgrown cotton dress switched about her calves, over the boot-tops. She kept her sleeves rolled up all day, and her arms and throat were burned as brown as a sailor's. Her neck came up strongly out of her shoulders, like the bole of a tree out of the turf. One sees that draught-horse neck among the peasant women in all old countries.

       She greeted me gaily, and began at once to tell me how much ploughing she had done that day. Ambrosch, she said, was on the north quarter, breaking sod with the oxen.

       "Jim, you ask Jake how much he ploughed to-day. I don't want that Jake get more done in one day than me. I want we have very much corn this fall."

       While the horses drew in the water, and nosed each other, and then drank again, Antonia sat down on the windmill step and rested her head on her hand.

Willa Cather

"You see the big prairie fire from your place last night? I hope your grandpa ain't lose no stacks?"

"No, we didn't. I came to ask you something, Tony. Grandmother wants to know if you can't go to the term of school that begins next week over at the sod school-house. She says there's a good teacher, and you'd learn a lot."

Antonia stood up, lifting and dropping her shoulders as if they were stiff. "I ain't got time to learn. I can work like mans now. My mother can't say no more how Ambrosch do all and nobody to help him. I can work as much as him. School is all right for little boys. I help make this land one good farm."

She clucked to her team and started for the barn. I walked beside her, feeling vexed. Was she going to grow up boastful like her mother, I wondered? Before we reached the stable, I felt something tense in her silence, and glancing up I saw that she was crying. She turned her face from me and looked off at the red streak of dying light, over the dark prairie.

I climbed up into the loft and threw down the hay for her, while she unharnessed her team. We walked slowly back toward the house. Ambrosch had come in from the north quarter, and was watering his oxen at the tank.

Antonia took my hand. "Sometime you will tell me all those nice things you learn at the school, won't you, Jimmy?" she asked with a sudden rush of feeling in her voice. "My father, he went much to school. He know a great deal; how to make the fine cloth like what you not got here. He play horn and violin, and he read so many books that the priests in

Bohemie come to talk to him. You won't forget my father, Jim?"

"No," I said, "I will never forget him."

Mrs. Shimerda asked me to stay for supper. After Ambrosch and Antonia had washed the field dust from their hands and faces at the wash-basin by the kitchen door, we sat down at the oilcloth-covered table. Mrs. Shimerda ladled meal mush out of an iron pot and poured milk on it. After the mush we had fresh bread and sorghum molasses, and coffee with the cake that had been kept warm in the feathers. Antonia and Ambrosch were talking in Bohemian; disputing about which of them had done more ploughing that day. Mrs. Shimerda egged them on, chuckling while she gobbled her food.

Presently Ambrosch said sullenly in English: "You take them ox to-morrow and try the sod plough. Then you not be so smart."

His sister laughed. "Don't be mad. I know it's awful hard work for break sod. I milk the cow for you to-morrow, if you want."

Mrs. Shimerda turned quickly to me. "That cow not give so much milk like what your grandpa say. If he make talk about fifteen dollars, I send him back the cow."

"He doesn't talk about the fifteen dollars," I exclaimed indignantly. "He doesn't find fault with people."

"He say I break his saw when we build, and I never," grumbled Ambrosch.

I knew he had broken the saw, and then hid it and lied about it. I began to wish I had not stayed for supper. Everything was disagreeable to me.

Antonia ate so noisily now, like a man, and she yawned often at the table and kept stretching her arms over her head, as if they ached. Grandmother had said, "Heavy field work'll spoil that girl. She'll lose all her nice ways and get rough ones." She had lost them already.

After supper I rode home through the sad, soft spring twilight. Since winter I had seen very little of Antonia. She was out in the fields from sunup until sundown. If I rode over to see her where she was ploughing, she stopped at the end of a row to chat for a moment, then gripped her plough-handles, clucked to her team, and waded on down the furrow, making me feel that she was now grown up and had no time for me. On Sundays she helped her mother make garden or sewed all day. Grandfather was pleased with Antonia. When we complained of her, he only smiled and said, "She will help some fellow get ahead in the world."

Nowadays Tony could talk of nothing but the prices of things, or how much she could lift and endure. She was too proud of her strength. I knew, too, that Ambrosch put upon her some chores a girl ought not to do, and that the farm-hands around the country joked in a nasty way about it. Whenever I saw her come up the furrow, shouting to her beasts, sunburned, sweaty, her dress open at the neck, and her throat and chest dust-plastered, I used to think of the tone in which poor Mr. Shimerda, who could say so little, yet managed to say so much when he exclaimed, "My Án-tonia!"

Colette

Colette

(1873–1954)

As a teenager, Sidonie Gabrielle Colette kicked up her French heels in the dance halls of Paris, an experience which provided her with bounteous material for the seventy works— plays, film scripts, reviews, short stories, and novels—that bore her maiden surname. One of France's most beloved female authors, she was also extremely prolific, despite the distractions of her gypsylike life. For example, *Gigi* (1943), about the initiation of a young girl into sensual and practical life by a family of prostitutes, was written while waiting for word of the fate of her second husband, a Jew whom the Germans had interred.

Best known for her portraits of indolent, jilted women of questionable virtue but virtuous intentions, Colette actually cast her dark-rimmed eyes on a variety of themes. Her first husband, a businessman, encouraged her to expand her journal jottings into real stories, and in 1900 she began publishing childhood memories and reflections about the natural world. Some novels, such as *Sido* (1929) and *My Mother's House* (1953), illustrate her fond vision of a mother figure who manages to make everything all right. In "The Sick Child," a short story in *The Tender Shoot* (1932), she writes of a boy who narrowly escapes death: "With a wave of his hand, Jean said farewell to his angel-haired reflection. The other returned his greeting from the depths of an earthly night short of all marvels, the only night allowed to children whom death lets go and who fall asleep, assenting, cured and disappointed."

The French are fond of saying that Colette created only three great women characters, reworking them throughout her literary career: a sensuous one based on herself, one a mother figure, and one a man-hungry prostitute. Indeed, it was her fascinating yarns about tainted women—albeit mature and proud ones who maintain civilized appearances and conduct their lives in a fashion that appears orderly and controlled—which brought Colette true acclaim. An example is Lea, the protagonist of Colette's celebrated novel *Cheri* (1920), about a lengthy *affaire d'amour* between a middle-aged woman and a greedy young (and not to mention married) gigolo named Cheri. Buoyed by its critical success, Colette created a sequel in 1926, *The Last of Cheri*, in which a world-weary Cheri returns after serving in World War I to find Lea an ordinary, elderly woman, no longer the sensual beauty of his fantasies. Deemed scandalous by some American critics, Colette's writing betrays no moral judgment on the circumstances, not even when she writes matter-of-factly of *menages a trois* and sexual androgyny.

At the end of her life, Colette described the aging process with unvarnished honesty. In *The Blue Lantern* (1949), a combination journal-memoir chronicling in exquisite detail how her life, once based on travel and passion, had so dwindled that it took place largely in one room, illuminated by the lamp of the title. "I am still going to write; I say this in all humility. For me there is no other destiny. But when does writing have an end? What is the warning sign? A trembling of the hand?" *The Blue Lantern* ends with the words "To be continued. . ."

In this selection from The Blue Lantern, *Colette turns her attention from the emotional roller-coaster of love to the simple pleasure of observing the world around her—in this case, a typical beach in the south of France.*

I am shown none but the most beautiful things. The kind attentions of my friends, never entirely devoid of humour, ensure that I am taken out for a drive of fifteen miles or so along the whole length of the Croisette, at the very time when among the concourse of bathers the nude figures of a man and a woman are on the point of clambering out of the water on to a float, at the precise moment when one man among a host of others in search of refreshment is staking his claim for a place at the pedestal table for himself and his fruit juice, where one bare back may be heard saying to the bare back beside it in a tone of defiance "But I tell you I've gone a far darker colour than you". I find the spectacle so strange that I insist, as at a merry-go-round, on having another turn.

Out at sea a boat is towing its pair of water-skis, for all the world like a silvery insect at the end of a line. In their coupled state, and lent enchantment by the distance, their pairing is the only one down here that evokes the idea of love. As for the rest . . . I do not believe I have ever seen a crowd less concerned with love, or so stripped to the buff, as this Cannes Vintage of 1948. They look just about as voluptuous as a keg of sardines, packed in their serried ranks. Let it be said, however, that here the weather is fine, whereas everywhere else it is raining. "Just one turn more?" I am granted it, driving along at a snail's pace between the sea and the dressmakers', the sea and the jewellers', the sea and the sandal-sellers, the vendors of brassières and fruit juices, the sea and hotels, cars, flowerstalls, sun-bathers and walnut-stained women. One yellow hotel has exceeded all reasonable proportions, making a mock of architectural harmony. An orchestra strives to make its feeble strains audible in the open air. I observe women who, in the guise of bathing costumes, wear creased or uncreased shorts of poor quality flowered fabrics and gorgerins like the hollows of one's hands. Such is their promenading attire of an afternoon; the hem above the thighs greasy and dirtied by oil. The men, in the security of a brief and highly revealing slip, give a far better account of themselves. No matter, there are far too many of them, men and women alike. "Would you care to take another turn?"—"No thanks!" I find it hard to tell whether all this varied display of human flesh is turning me into a vegetarian, or whether I am shockingly jealous of those who apparently derive pleasure from their own agility, the briny, and going naked.

The realities of an intimate companion's flesh and blood are almost too much to bear for the young bride in Colette's short-short story "The Hand" (1924), printed here in its entirety. Colette tempers the bride's loving ambivalence wih her own rather dim view of marriage as a lowly, delicate diplomacy.

He had fallen asleep on his young wife's shoulder, and she proudly supported the weight of his head, with its fair hair, his sanguine-complexioned face and closed eyes. He had slipped his large arm beneath the slim, adolescent back and his strong hand lay flat on the sheet, beside the young woman's right elbow. She smiled as she looked at the man's hand emerging there, quite alone and far removed from its owner. Then she let her glance stray round the dimly lit bedroom. A conch-shaped lamp threw a subdued glow of periwinkle-blue over the bed. "Too happy to sleep," she thought.

Too excited also, and often surprised by her new state. For only two weeks she had taken part in the scandalous existence of a honeymoon couple, each of them relishing the pleasure of living with an unknown person they were in love with. To meet a good-looking, fair-haired young man, recently widowed, good at tennis and sailing, and marry him a month later: her conjugal romance fell little short of abduction. Whenever she lay awake beside her husband, like tonight, she would still keep her eyes closed for a long time, then open them and relish with astonishment the blue of the brand-new curtains, replacing the apricot-pink which had filtered with the morning light into the room where she had slept as a girl.

A shudder ran through the sleeping body lying beside her and she tightened her left arm round her husband's neck, with the delightful authority of weak creatures. He did not wake up.

"What long eyelashes he has," she said to herself.

She silently praised also the full, graceful

mouth, the brick-red skin and the forehead, neither noble nor lofty, but still free of wrinkles.

Her husband's right hand, beside her, also shuddered, and beneath the curve of her back she felt the right arm, on which her whole weight was resting, come to life.

"I'm heavy . . . I'd like to reach up and put the light out, but he's so fast asleep. . . ."

The arm tensed again, gently, and she arched her back to make herself lighter.

"It's as though I were lying on an animal," she thought.

She turned her head slightly on the pillow and looked at the hand lying beside her.

"How big it is! It's really bigger than my whole head!"

The light which crept from under the edge of a blue crystal globe fell on to this hand and showed up the slightest reliefs in the skin, exaggerated the powerful, knotty knuckles and the veins which stood out because of the pressure on the arm. A few russet hairs, at the base of the fingers, all lay in the same direction, like ears of wheat in the wind, and the flat nails, whose ridges had not been smoothed out by the polisher, gleamed beneath their coat of pink varnish.

"I'll tell him not to put varnish on his nails," thought the young wife. "Varnish and carmine don't suit a hand so . . . a hand so . . ."

An electric shock ran through the hand and spared the young woman the trouble of thinking of an adjective. The thumb stiffened until it was horribly long and spatulate, and moved close up against the index finger. In this way the hand suddenly acquired an apelike appearance.

"Oh!" said the young woman quietly, as though faced with some minor indecency.

The horn of a passing car pierced the silence with a noise so shrill that it seemed luminous. The sleeper did not wake but the hand seemed offended and reared up, tensing itself like a crab and waiting for the fray. The piercing sound receded and the hand, gradually relaxing, let fall its claws, became a soft animal, bent double and shaken with faint jerks which looked like a death agony. The flat, cruel nail on the over-long thumb glistened. On the little finger there appeared a slight deviation which the young woman had never noticed, and the sprawling hand revealed its fleshy palm like a red belly.

"And I've kissed that hand! . . . How horrible! I can't ever have looked at it!"

The hand was disturbed by some bad dream, and seemed to respond to this sudden reaction, this disgust. It regrouped its forces, opened out wide, spread out its tendons, its nerves and its hairiness like a panoply of war. Then it slowly withdrew, grasped a piece of sheeting, dug down with its curving fingers and squeezed and squeezed with the methodical pleasure of a strangler. . . .

"Oh!" cried the young woman.

The hand disappeared, the large arm was freed of its burden and in one moment became a protective girdle, a warm bulwark against the terrors of night. But next morning, when the tray with frothing chocolate and toast was on the bed, she saw the hand again, russet and red, and the ghastly thumb crooked over the handle of a knife.

"Do you want this piece of toast, darling? I'm doing it for you."

She shuddered and felt gooseflesh high up on her arms and down her back.

"Oh, no . . . no . . ."

Then she concealed her fear, controlled herself bravely and, beginning her life of duplicity, resignation, base and subtle diplomacy, she leant over and humbly kissed the monstrous hand.

Gertrude Stein

Gertrude Stein

(1874–1946)

"Gertrude Stein, in her work, has always been possessed by the intellectual passion for exactitude in her description of inner and outer reality," wrote Gertrude Stein in *The Autobiography of Alice B. Toklas*. Pleased with her own cleverness, she became a legendary figure in her own time while realizing, with regret, that her experiments in poetry were little understood or appreciated by the reading public at large.

"You have to learn to do everything, even to die," she once commented with typical tragicomic irony. Born in Allegheny, Pennsylvania to a wealthy Jewish-Bavarian family, Stein took for granted the luxury of time and money to spend learning. She grew up in northern California, New York City, and Baltimore, before leaving her parents' home to study psychology at Radcliffe. In that liberated environment, she bobbed her hair and wrote a daring Freshman English essay called "In the Red Deeps," a hallucination by a young woman afraid of madness and sadomasochism. She precociously took the title from a chapter title in George Eliot's *The Mill on the Floss*.

Stein went on to study medicine at Johns Hopkins University but left before receiving a degree. She and her brother Leo moved to Paris in 1903, never to live in the U.S. again. It was in the heady, creative atmosphere of the bohemian Left Bank that she established her famous salon, where Apollinaire, Picasso, Hemingway, Fitzgerald, and Laurencin gathered for tea, sympathy, and brilliant discussion. At the same time, she and Leo began amassing their famous collection of paintings with the works of Cezanne and Matisse. Her association with members of the Cubist school, headed by Picasso and Juan Gris, became one of the prime influences in her writing, and she attempted to express in words the ideas of the painters who flocked to her parlor.

Always present was Alice B. Toklas, Stein's lifelong companion, whose charming, Franco-modernist cookbook remains an inspiration to culinarily inclined readers. The two traveled to Spain and elsewhere through Europe, with Stein recording details of the people they met, complete with their quirks and foibles, while Alice took care of them both. Stein's *Autobiography of Alice B. Toklas* (1932) is an oblique yet revealing look at their lives together as colleagues and lovers. Oblique, yet revealing if you knew where to look—that's how most people take the desperately intelligent, wildly clever work of Stein. Her famous line "a rose is a rose is a rose" demonstrates her dual talent for seducing and confusing.

Stein's first published work was *Three Lives* (1909), about the artists whose ideas she championed, followed by the astonishing *Tender Buttons* (1914), a prose-poem influenced by the Cubist movement. *The Making of Americans* (1925) is an epic novel that betrays Stein's psychological training in human behavior studies. Her experiences in France during World War II are recorded in *Wars I Have Seen* (1942-44). Stein died of inoperable cancer in a hospital in the countryside, with Alice B. Toklas by her side.

The curiously seductive repetition that characterizes much of Stein's work appears in this excerpt about her motivation for writing from The Making of Americans.

I am writing for myself and strangers. This is the only way that I can do it. Everybody is a real one to me, everybody is like some one else too to me. No one of them that I know can want to know it and so I write for myself and strangers.

Every one is always busy with it, no one of them then ever want to know it that every one looks like some one else and they see it. Mostly every one dislikes to hear it. It is very important to me to always know it, to always see it which one looks like others and to tell it. I write for myself and strangers. I do this for my own sake and for the sake of those who know I know it that they look like other ones, that they are separate and yet always repeated. There are some who like it that I know they are like many others and repeat it, there are many who never can really like it.

There are many that I know and they know it. They are all of them repeating and I hear it. I love it and I tell it, I love it and now I will write it. This is now the history of the way some of them are it.

I write for myself and strangers. No one who knows me can like it. At least they mostly do not like it that every one is of a kind of men and women and I see it. I love it and I write it.

I want readers so strangers must do it. Mostly no one knowing me can like it that I love it that every one is a kind of men and women, that always I am looking and comparing and classifying of them, always I am seeing their repeating. Always more and more I love repeating, it may be irritating to hear from them but always more and more I love it of them. More and more I love it of them, the being in them, the mixing in them, the repeating in them, the deciding the kind of them every one is who has human being.

This is now a little of what I love and how I write it. Later there will be much more of it.

There are many ways of making kinds of men and women. Now there will be descriptions of every kind of way every one can be a kind of men and women.

This is now a history of Martha Hersland. This is now a history of Martha and of every one who came to be of her living.

There will then be soon much description of every way one can think of men and women, in their beginning, in their middle living, and their ending.

Every one then is an individual being. Every one then is like many others always living, there are many ways of thinking of every one, this is now a description of all of them. There must then be a whole history of each one of them. There must now be a description of all repeating. Now I will tell all the meaning to me in repeating, the loving there is in me for repeating.

Stein provides a tongue-in-cheek description of herself in The Autobiography of Alice B. Toklas, *which Stein wrote about her life-long companion.*

Before I decided to write this book on my twenty-five years with Gertrude Stein, I had often said that I would write, The wives of geniuses I have sat with. I have sat with so many. I have sat with wives who were not wives, of geniuses who were real geniuses. I have sat with real wives of geniuses who were not real geniuses. I have sat with wives of geniuses, of near geniuses, of would be geniuses, in short I have sat very often and very long with many wives and wives of many geniuses.

As I was saying Fernande, who was then living with Picasso and had been with him a long time that is to say they were all twenty-four years old at that time but they had been together a long time, Fernande was the first wife of a genius I sat with and she was not the least amusing. We talked hats. Fernande

had two subjects hats and perfumes. This first day we talked hats. She liked hats, she had the true french feeling about a hat, if a hat did not provoke some witticism from a man on the street the hat was not a success. Later on once in Montmartre she and I were walking together. She had on a large yellow hat and I had on a much smaller blue one. As we were walking along a workman stopped and called out, there go the sun and the moon shining together. Ah, said Fernande to me with a radiant smile, you see our hats are a success.

Miss Stein called me and said she wanted to have me meet Matisse. She was talking to a medium sized man with a reddish beard and glasses. He had a very alert although slightly heavy presence and Miss Stein and he seemed to be full of hidden meanings.

As I came up I heard her say, Oh yes but it would be more difficult now. We were talking, she said, of a lunch party we had in here last year. We had just hung all the pictures and we asked all the painters. You know how painters are, I wanted to make them happy so I placed each one opposite his own picture, and they were happy so happy that we had to send out twice for more bread, when you know France you will know that that means that they were happy, because they cannot eat and drink without bread and we had to send out twice for bread so they were happy. Nobody noticed my little arrangement except Matisse and he did not until just as he left, and now he says it is a proof that I am very wicked, Matisse laughed and said, yes I know Mademoiselle Gertrude, the world is a theatre for you, but there are theatres and theatres, and when you listen so carefully to me and so attentively and do not hear a word I say then I do say that you are very wicked. Then they both began talking about the vernissage of the independent as every one else was doing and of course I did not know what it was all about. But gradually I knew and later on I will tell the story of the pictures, their painters and their followers and what this conversation meant.

Virginia Woolf

(1882–1941)

*A*deline Virginia Stephen seemed destined for the literary life. She was born in London to Sir Leslie Stephen, an esteemed intellectual and writer, and his second wife, Julia Duckworth. Virginia, as she was known, was a dyed-in-the-wool aristocrat raised to take life's finer aspects for granted. She was only a young adult when she declared that "One cannot think well, love well, sleep well, if one has not dined well."

While still in her early twenties, Virginia founded the Bloomsbury Group, an informal alliance based on friendship and interest in the arts, with her sister and brothers. She soon began what was to become a lifelong association as a contributor to London's *Times Literary Supplement.* Virginia was already at work on her first novel, *The Voyage Out,* when she married the writer and social reformer Leonard Woolf in 1912. Five years later, the couple established the Hogarth Press, dedicated to publishing the works of contemporary authors as well as translations of such esteemed foreign writers as Chekov, Dostoevsky, and Rilke.

Woolf herself evolved into one of the century's most innovative writers, employing such then-exotic techniques as stream of consciousness, indirect narration, and poetic impressionism. She was also a literary critic whose sharp-witted essays on subjects ranging from John Donne to Mary Wollstonecraft to Thomas Hardy were collected in several volumes, including two called *The Common Reader.* A published attack on the use of realism in novels, championing her own use of less structured narrative, established Woolf as a major figure in the Modernist literary movement.

Woolf not only worked tirelessly at journalism, criticism, and fiction, but also kept prodigious diaries and wrote thousands of letters. Madness in varying degrees of severity was a common theme in her literary labors, and in Woolf's case, art imitated life. She suffered bouts

Virginia Woolf

of mental distress and was particularly affected by the deaths of her mother and her brother Thoby, the latter inspiring the novel *Jacob's Room* (1922). Virginia finally succumbed to depression at the age of 59 when she filled her pockets with rocks and drowned herself.

Woolf's thoughtful examinations of women's places in society and their relationships with men went beyond her contemporaries's passions for "mere" suffragism. In her landmark essay *A Room of One's Own* (1929), she pondered the obstacles that might have confronted Shakespeare's hypothetical sister had she been seized by her renowned sibling's desire to write drama. Woolf noted that throughout history, women had been married against their wills, forced to bear more children than they wanted, and deprived of both education and privacy—all nigh-insurmountable obstacles to the writing life.

When women *could* write, Woolf believed, they found themselves lacking men's grand tradition of predecessors, with no classics of their own to emulate. Today, the legacy of this brilliant, troubled woman provides female writers with rich inspiration in both form and content, as well as passion for putting down words on a blank page.

In her famous essay about women and writing entitled A Room of One's Own, *Woolf candidly explains how an unexpected inheritance affords her the independence to live comfortably as a writer.*

My aunt, Mary Beton, I must tell you, died by a fall from her horse when she was riding out to take the air in Bombay. The news of my legacy reached me one night about the same time that the act was passed that gave votes to women. A solicitor's letter fell into the post-box and when I opened it I found that she had left me five hundred pounds a year for ever. Of the two—the vote and the money—the money, I own, seemed infinitely the more important. Before that I had made my living by cadging odd jobs from newspapers, by reporting a donkey show here or a wedding there; I had earned a few pounds by addressing envelopes, reading to old ladies, making artificial flowers, teaching the alphabet to small children in a kindergarten. Such were the chief occupations that were open to women before 1918. I need not, I am afraid, describe in any detail the hardness of the work, for you know perhaps women who have done it; nor the difficulty of living on the money when it was earned, for you may have tried. But what still remains with me as a worse infliction than either was the poison of fear and bitterness which those days bred in me. To begin with, always to be doing work that one did not wish to do, and to do it like a slave, flattering and fawning, not always necessarily perhaps, but it seemed necessary and the stakes were too great to run risks; and then the thought of that one gift which it was death to hide—a small one but dear to the possessor—perishing and with it myself, my soul—all this became like a rust eating away the bloom of the spring, destroying the tree at its heart. However, as I say, my aunt died; and whenever I change a ten-shilling note a little of that rust and corrosion is rubbed off; fear and bitterness go. Indeed, I thought, slipping the silver into my purse, it is remarkable, remembering the bitterness of those days, what a change of temper a fixed income will bring about. No force in the world can take from me my five hundred pounds. Food, house and clothing are mine for ever. Therefore not merely do effort and labour cease, but also hatred and bitterness. I need not hate any man; he cannot hurt me. I need not flatter any man; he has nothing to give me. So imperceptibly I found myself adopting a new attitude towards the other half of the human race. It was absurd to blame any class or any sex, as a whole. Great bodies of people are never responsible for what they do. They are driven by instincts which are not within their control. They too, the patriarchs, the professors, had endless difficulties, terrible drawbacks to contend with. Their education had been in some ways as faulty as my own. It had bred in them defects as great. True, they had money and power, but only at the cost of harbouring in their breasts an eagle, a vulture, for ever tearing the liver out and plucking at the lungs—the instinct for possession, the rage for acquisition which drives them to desire other people's fields and goods perpetually; to make frontiers and flags; battleships and poison gas; to offer up their own lives and their children's lives. Walk through the Admiralty Arch (I had reached that monument), or any other avenue given up to trophies and cannon, and reflect upon the kind of glory celebrated there. Or watch in the spring sunshine the stockbroker and the great barrister going indoors to make money and more money and more money when it is a fact that five hundred pounds a year will keep one alive in the sunshine. These are unpleasant instincts to harbour, I reflected. They are bred of the conditions of life; of the lack of civilisation, I thought, looking at the statue of the Duke of Cambridge, and in particular at the feathers in his cocked hat, with a fixity that they have scarcely ever received before. And, as I realised these drawbacks, by degrees fear and bitterness modified themselves into pity and toleration; and then in a year or two, pity and toleration went, and the greatest release of all came, which is freedom to think of things in themselves. That building, for example, do I like it or not? Is that picture beautiful or not? Is that in my opinion a good book or a bad? Indeed my aunt's legacy unveiled the sky to me, and substituted for the large and imposing figure of a gentleman, which Milton recommended for my perpetual adoration, a view of the open sky.

Woolf offers readers perhaps the wisest advice ever in her essay How Should One Read a Book?: *put down the volume in your hand, try writing a paragraph yourself, and then return to the book, with new appreciation for the author's craft.*

It is simple enough to say that since books have classes—fiction, biography, poetry—we should separate them and take from each what it is right that each should give us. Yet few people ask from books what books can give us. Most commonly we come to books with blurred and divided minds, asking of fiction that it shall be true, of poetry that it shall be false, of biography that it shall be flattering, of history that it shall enforce our own prejudices. If we could banish all such preconceptions when we read, that would be an admirable beginning. Do not dictate to your author; try to become him. Be his fellow-worker and accomplice. If you hang back, and reserve and criticise at first, you are preventing yourself from getting the fullest possible value from what you read. But if you open your mind as widely as possible, then signs and hints of almost imperceptible fineness, from the twist and turn of the first sentences, will bring you into the presence of a human being unlike any other. Steep yourself in this, acquaint yourself with this, and soon you will find that your author is giving you, or attempting to give you, something far more definite. The thirty-chapters of a novel—if we consider how to read a novel first—are an attempt to make something as formed and controlled as a building: but words are more impalpable than bricks; reading is a longer and more complicated process than seeing. Perhaps the quickest way to understand the elements of what a novelist is doing is not to read, but to write; to make your own experiment with the dangers and difficulties of words. Recall, then, some event that has left a distinct impression on you—how at the corner of the street, perhaps, you passed two people talking. A tree shook; an electric light danced; the tone of the talk was comic, but also tragic; a whole vision, an entire conception, seemed contained in that moment.

But when you attempt to reconstruct it in words, you will find that it breaks into a thousand conflicting impressions. Some must be subdued; others emphasised; in the process you will lose, probably, all grasp upon the emotion itself. Then turn from your blurred and littered pages to the opening of some great novelist—Defoe, Jane Austen, Hardy. Now you will be better able to appreciate their mastery.

Isak Dinesen

Isak Dinesen

(1885–1962)

*A*t various times in her life, Karen Christentze Dinesen answered to the names Isak ("one who laughs"), Baroness von Blixen-Finecke (her title by marriage), and Pierre Andrezel, a pseudonym. It was as Isak Dinesen that the adventuresome writer staked her place on the great time line of literature.

Born in Rungsted, Denmark, to an upper-class family, she wrote plays and stories as a child, and later sold articles to local publications. Soon after enrolling in Oxford University to study English, Dinesen rebelled against her bourgeois upbringing and went to Copenhagen, Paris, and Rome to become a painter. In 1914, back in Denmark, she married her cousin, Baron Bror Blixen-Finecke. They traveled to the Kenyan hills, in what was then British East Africa, to establish a coffee plantation.

The baron may have been a renowned wild game hunter, but he proved to be both a bad businessman and an unfaithful husband. As a result of the latter, Dinesen was stricken with such a severe case of syphilis that she was forced to retreat to Denmark to recuperate. The disease, which plagued her throughout her life, also dashed her hope of having children. Though the marriage ended in 1921, Africa remained in Dinesen's heart, and she returned to manage the plantation with the help of her brother. Finally, the collapse of the coffee market forced her to sell her beloved property and return, penniless, to Denmark in 1931. There she began to write, in English, under the Dinesen name.

When she translated her first book, *Seven Gothic Tales* (1934) into Danish, it became a literary success that allowed Dinesen to resume her aristocratic lifestyle. A Danish critic of the time pointed out that "there are no normal human beings" in these tales. Indeed, the characters—barons, countesses, and others of Dinesen's social milieu—are involved in fantastic erotic, psychic, and psychological situations. *Seven Gothic Tales* echoes the "decadent" writings of the French Symbolists, such as Baudelaire, whose work Dinesen admired.

Her greatest success was *Out of Africa* (1937), a lyrical, autobiographical saga of a regal foreign woman who establishes a farm in Kenya. Without so much as a mention of the man who brought her there, Dinesen portrays herself as an accomplished hunter, a savvy hostess to such raffish characters as her real-life lover, British aviator Denys Finch-Hatton (who died in a plane crash), and a benevolent diplomat at ease with the Kikuyu natives who worked for her.

After demystifying and romanticizing the Dark Continent in *Out of Africa*, Dinesen wrote numerous short stories and published a handful of other books, including *Winter's Tales* (1942), *Angelic Avengers* (1944, written under the Andrezel pseudonym), and *Last Tales*, issued after her death. During her African heyday, Dinesen had been a fabulous hostess who enjoyed spoiling her guests with the finest dinners. In 1949 she sold a story about just such a woman to the American magazine *Ladies' Home Journal*. Entitled "Babette's Feast," it serves as an eloquent illustration of the way in which Dinesen's intriguing life continued to nourish her literary imagination, long after her days at the head of a glittering table had come to an end.

Dinesen had many adventures while living on her Kenyan coffee plantation. However, it was not until she met the dashing explorer Denys Finch-Hatton that she had the chance to fly in an airplane and view her beloved country from a thrilling new vantage point, which she describes in Out of Africa.

To Denys Finch-Hatton I owe what was, I think, the greatest, the most transporting pleasure of my life on the farm: I flew with him over Africa. There, where there are few or no roads and where you can land on the plains, flying becomes a thing of real and vital importance in your life, it opens up a world. Denys had brought out his Moth machine; it could land on my plain on the farm only a few minutes from the house, and we were up nearly every day.

You have tremendous views as you get up above the African highlands, surprising combinations and changes of light and colouring, the rainbow on the green sunlit land, the gigantic upright clouds and big wild black storms, all swing round you in a race and a dance. The lashing hard showers of rain whiten the air askance. The language is short of words for the experiences of flying, and will have to invent new words with time. When you have flown over the Rift Valley and the volcanoes of Suswa and Longonot, you have travelled far and have been to the lands on the other side of the moon. You may at other times fly low enough to see the animals on the plains and to feel towards them as God did when he had just created them, and before he commissioned Adam to give them names.

But it is not the visions but the activity

which makes you happy, and the joy and glory of the flyer is the flight itself. It is a sad hardship and slavery to people who live in towns, that in all their movements they know of one dimension only; they walk along the line as if they were led on a string. The transition from the line to the plane into the two dimensions, when you wander across a field or through a wood, is a splendid liberation to the slaves, like the French Revolution. But in the air you are taken into the full freedom of the three dimensions; after long ages of exile and dreams the homesick heart throws itself into the arms of space. The laws of gravitation and time,

> "... in life's green grove,
> Sport like tame beasts, none knew how
> gentle they could be!"

Every time that I have gone up in an aeroplane and looking down have realised that I was free of the ground, I have had the consciousness of a great new discovery. "I see:" I have thought, "This was the idea. And now I understand everything."

One day Denys and I flew to Lake Natron, ninety miles South-East of the farm, and more than four thousand feet lower, two thousand feet above Sea level. Lake Natron is the place from where they take soda. The bottom of the lake and the shores are like some sort of whitish concrete, with a strong, sour and salt smell.

The sky was blue, but as we flew from the plains in over the stony and bare lower country, all colour seemed to be scorched out of it. The whole landscape below us looked like delicately marked tortoise-shell. Suddenly, in the midst of it was the lake. The white bottom, shining through the water, gives it, when seen from the air, a striking, an unbelievable azure-colour, so clear that for a moment you shut your eyes at it; the expanse of water lies in the bleak tawny land like a big bright aquamarine. We had been flying high, now we went down, and as we sank our own shade, dark-blue, floated under us upon the light-blue lake. Here live thousands of Flamingoes, although I do not know how they exist in the brackish water,—surely there are no fish here. At our approach they spread out in large circles and fans, like the rays of a setting sun, like an artful Chinese pattern on silk or porcelain, forming itself and changing, as we looked at it.

We landed on the white shore, that was white-hot as an oven, and lunched there, taking shelter against the sun under the wing of the aeroplane. If you stretched out your hand from the shade, the sun was so hot that it hurt you. Our bottles of beer when they first arrived with us, straight out of the ether, were pleasantly cold, but before we had finished them, in a quarter of an hour, they became as hot as a cup of tea.

While we were lunching, a party of Masai warriors appeared on the horizon, and approached quickly. They must have spied the aeroplane landing from a distance, and resolved to have a close look at it, and a walk of any length, even in a country like this, means nothing to a Masai. They came along, the one in front of the other, naked, tall and narrow, their weapons glinting; dark like peat on the yellow grey sand. At the feet of each of them lay and marched a small pool of shadow, these were, besides our own, the only shadows in the country as far as the eye reached. When they came up to us they fell in line, there were five of them. They struck their heads together and began to talk to one another about the aeroplane and us. A generation ago they would have been fatal to us to meet. After a time one of them advanced and spoke to us. As they could only speak Masai and we understood but little of the language, the conversation soon slackened, he stepped back to his fellows and a few minutes later they all turned their back upon us, and walked away, in single file, with the wide white burning salt-plain before them.

"Would you care," said Denys, "to fly to Naivasha? But the country lying between is very rough, we could not possibly land anywhere on the way. So we shall have to go up high and keep up at twelve thousand feet."

The flight from Lake Natron to Naivasha was *Das ding an sich*. We took a bee-line, and kept at twelve thousand feet all the way, which is so high that there is nothing to look down for. At Lake Natron I had taken off my lamb-skin-lined cap, now up here the air squeezed my forehead, as cold as iced water; all my hair flew backwards as if my head was being pulled off. This path, in fact, was the same as was, in the opposite direction, every evening taken by the Roc, when, with an Elephant for her young in each talon, she swished from Uganda home to Arabia. Where you are sitting in front of your pilot, with nothing but space before you, you feel that he is carrying you upon the outstretched palms of his hands, as the Djinn carried Prince Ali through the air, and that the wings that bear you onward are his.

Marianne Moore

(1887–1972)

An only child, Marianne Moore never really got to know her father. He was hospitalized for mental illness after the family moved from St. Louis, Missouri, Moore's birthplace, to western Pennsylvania and did not recover. Moore was raised by her mother, who worked to support the two of them. As a result, the poet grew up with a somber wisdom that was to influence her choices of subject matter later in life.

A talented student, Moore graduated from Bryn Mawr College in 1909 with a degree in biology and histology. Although she longed to become a painter, she chose a more practical pursuit: teaching stenography at a government-run Indian school in Carlisle, Pennsylvania. When she was thirty-one, Moore moved with her mother to New York City, where she worked as a secretary, tutor, and Public Library clerk.

But in 1921, Moore's life began to change. Two of her friends—fellow poets Annie Winifred Ellerman, who wrote under the name Bryher, and Hilda Doolittle, alias H.D.—submitted Moore's work to Egoist Press, a London publisher, without her knowledge. The result was a collection entitled *Poems*. The same year, Moore became editor of the transcendentalist magazine *Dial*, founded by Ralph Waldo Emerson, and remained until its demise in 1929.

Moore incorporated her passions for politics and animals into her work, and romantic love had no place in her poetry. Literary inspiration was as likely to come from high-minded conversations with the poets Wallace Stevens and William Carlos Williams as from afternoons spent at the Bronx Zoo, observing the interaction of a pair of tigers.

Dissatisfied with traditional poetic forms, Moore turned contemporary poetry on its ear. Experimenting with the layered sounds of the English language, she turned a watchful eye

Marianne Moore

on the wild, natural world around her: "The whirlwind fife-and-drum of the storm bends the salt marsh grass, disturbs stars in the sky and the star on the steeple; it is a privilege to see so much confusion," she observed in "The Steeple-Jack" (1924; revised 1964). Moore also wrote two volumes of literary criticism, and translated the *Fables* of the Frenchman Jean de La Fontaine, charming stories about garden snails, exotic birds, and other creatures.

Baseball was another of her lifelong loves. Moore, a Brooklyn Dodgers fan, once remarked to an acquaintance that she would have liked to have been the one who invented the "eight-shaped stitch with which the outer leather is drawn tight on a baseball."

Collected Poems (1952) earned Moore the National Book Award, the Pulitzer Prize, and the Bollingen Prize—the three highest honors in American verse writing. She had once written about her calling: "I, too, dislike it: there are things that are important beyond all this fiddle." Perhaps she did, perhaps not. For in 1968, four years before her death at the age of eighty-five, she tossed out the first ball on Opening Day at Yankee Stadium. One can't help but feel that in Moore's own eyes, that was her finest hour.

The sea has inspired poets for centuries, but Moore, never one to romanticize, takes a pragmatic look at it as the most impersonal of final resting places in her 1924 poem "A Grave." Perhaps her most famous work, "Poetry" (1921) is Moore's cool, unromantic appraisal of her chosen field.

A Grave

Man looking into the sea,
   taking the view from those who have as much
     right to it as you have to yourself,
it is human nature to stand in the middle of a thing,
but you cannot stand in the middle of this;
the sea has nothing to give but a well excavated grave.
The firs stand in a procession, each with an emerald
     turkey-foot at the top,
reserved as their contours, saying nothing;
repression, however, is not the most obvious charac-
     teristic of the sea;

the sea is a collector, quick to return a rapacious
     look.
There are others besides you who have worn that
     look—
whose expression is no longer a protest; the fish no
     longer investigate them
for their bones have not lasted:
men lower nets, unconscious of the fact that they are
     desecrating a grave,
and row quickly away—the blades of the oars
moving together like the feet of water-spiders as if
     there were no such thing as death.
The wrinkles progress among themselves in a
     phalanx—beautiful under networks of foam,

and fade breathlessly while the sea rustles in and out
of the seaweed;
the birds swim through the air at top speed, emitting
catcalls as heretofore—
the tortoise-shell scourges about the feet of the cliffs,
in motion beneath them;
and the ocean, under the pulsation of lighthouses and
noise of bell-buoys,
advances as usual, looking as if it were not that ocean
in which dropped things are bound to sink—
in which if they turn and twist, it is neither with
volition nor consciousness.

Poetry

I too, dislike it: there are things that are important
beyond all this fiddle.
Reading it, however, with a perfect contempt for it
one discovers in it after all, a place for the genuine.
Hands that can grasp, eyes
that can dilate, hair that can rise
if it must, these things are important not
because a
high-sounding interpretation can be put upon them
but because they are
useful. When they become so derivative as to
become unintelligible,
the same thing may be said for all of us, that we
do not admire what
we cannot understand: the bat

holding on upside down or in quest of some
thing to

eat, elephants pushing, a wild horse taking a roll, a
tireless wolf under
a tree, the immovable critic twitching his skin like
a horse that feels a flea, the base-
ball fan, the statistician—
nor is it valid
to discriminate against 'business documents
and

school-books'; all these phenomena are important.
One must make a distinction
however: when dragged into prominence by half
poets, the result is not poetry,
nor till the poets among us can be
'literalists of
the imagination'—above
insolence and triviality and can present

for inspection, 'imaginary gardens with real toads in
them', shall we have
it. In the meantime, if you demand on the one
hand,
the raw material of poetry in
all its rawness and
that which is on the other hand
genuine, you are interested in poetry.

Edith Sitwell

(1887–1964)

"**M**y parents were strangers to me from the moment of my birth," wrote the first child of baronet Sir George and Lady Ida Sitwell. Exceptionally tall and considered quite unattractive by the standards of the day, Edith Sitwell rebelled at an early age against the social conventions of the aristocratic world into which she had been born. At Renishaw Hall, the family estate outside London, her childhood misery was made bearable by the company of her brothers, Osbert and Sacheverell, who also became writers.

As young adults, the three Sitwells were united in their contempt for Georgian poetry, the literary fashion of the day. Edith was fond of referring to those who wrote the pastoral, "escapist" verse popular during the reign of George V (1910–1936) as "dim bucolics," characterizing it as the work of "verbal deadness, the dead and expected patterns." She was writing poetry of a very different nature, influenced by the Modernist movement, which took its inspiration from the relatively new disciplines of anthropology and Freudian psychology. "Drowned Suns," her first poem, appeared in the *Daily Mirror* in 1913. *The Mother and Other Poems* (1915), a poetry collection, was followed by many others.

Edith's reputation as an eccentric was cemented when, from 1916 to 1921, she edited *Wheels*, an anti-Georgian literary magazine. Other writers called her a controversialist. The music of Stravinsky, the Russian ballet of Diaghilev, and modern art stirred her creative urges.

Sitwell's *modus operandi* as a writer was experimentation. She created innovative poetry based on musical forms, exemplified in the abstract *Facade* (1920) and *Gold Coast Customs* (1929). *Facade* was performed in 1923 at Aeolian Hall in London, set to music by William Walton, its verses presented in syncopated rhythms. *Gold Coast Customs*, by comparison, was a

Edith Sitwell

harshly satirical criticism of modern European society, which Sitwell compared to the ancient barbarian cultures of Africa. She also did some writing "to pay the rent," including a 1930 study of the British poet Alexander Pope.

As Sitwell aged, her interest in prophecy grew, though she maintained a strong belief in Christianity. Her poems, she wrote, were "hymns of praise to the glory of life." Sitwell's only novel, *I Live Under a Black Sun* (1937) was poorly received. However, she received great acclaim when she began writing about political events—the blitz and the atom bomb—in such poetry volumes as *Street Song* (1942), and *The Song of the Cold* (1945). Queen Elizabeth II pronounced her a Dame Grand Cross of the British Empire.

In the postwar era, Edith Sitwell's reputation began to fade, but she remained a fascinating public figure who affected a theatrical mode of dress and ebullient manner. Her offbeat looks were suddenly in vogue among artists and photographers. She received honorary degrees from Oxford, Cambridge, and other institutions, and toured the United States giving poetry readings to great fanfare. By that time the Beatnik poets were beginning to write in America, and in her unlikely way, Edith Sitwell had helped them find their voices.

"The Poet Laments the Coming of Old Age" (1945) is Sitwell's solemn commentary on the grand inevitability of life, influenced as much by Platonic dialogue as by the schoolchildren she observes at play. Glorious language and fantastic imagery make "Country Dance" (1923) delightful to read aloud.

The Poet Laments the Coming of Old Age

I see the children running out of school;
They are taught that Goodness means a blinding
    hood
Or is heaped by Time like the hump on an agèd
    back,
And that Evil can be cast like an old rag
And Wisdom caught like a hare and held in the
    golden sack
Of the heart. . . . But I am one who must bring back
    sight to the blind.

Yet there was a planet dancing in my mind
With a gold seed of Folly . . . long ago. . . .
And where is that grain of Folly? . . . with the hare-
    wild wind
Of my spring it has gone from one who must bring
    back sight to the blind.

For I, the fool, was once like the philosopher
Sun who laughs at evil and at good:
I saw great things mirrored in littleness,
Who now see only that great Venus wears Time's
    filthy dress—
A toothless crone who once had the Lion's mouth.

The Gold Appearances from Nothing rise
In sleep, by day . . . . Two thousands years ago
There was a man who had the Lion's leap,
Like the Sun's, to take the worlds and loves he
    would,
But (laughed the philosopher Sun, and I, the fool)

Great golden Alexander and his thunder-store
Are now no more
Than the armored knight who buzzed on the
    windowpane
And the first drops of rain.

He lies in sleep . . . But still beneath a thatch
Of hair like sunburnt grass, the thieving sweet
    thoughts move
Towards the honey-hive. . . . And another sweet-
    tooth Alexander runs
Out of the giant shade that is his school,
To take the dark knight's world, the honeycomb.

The Sun's simulacrum, the gold-sinewed man,
Lies under a hump of grass, as once I thought to
    wear
With patience Goodness like a hump on my agèd
    back.
. . . But Goodness grew not with age, although my
    heart must bear
The weight of all Time's filth, and Wisdom is not a
    hare in the golden sack

Of the heart. . . . It can never be caught. Though I
    bring back sight to the blind,
My seed of Folly has gone, that could teach me to
    bear
That the gold-sinewed body that had the blood of all
    the earth in its veins
Has changed to an old rag of the outworn world
And the great heart that the first Morning made
Should wear all Time's destruction for a dress.

Country Dance

That hobnailed goblin, the bobtailed Hob,
Said, "It is time I began to rob."
For strawberries bob, hob-nob with the pearls
Of cream (like the curls of the dairy girls),
And flushed with the heat and fruitish-ripe
Are the gowns of the maids who dance to the pipe.
Chase a maid?
She's afraid!
"Go gather a bob-cherry kiss from a tree,
But don't, I prithee, come bothering me!"
She said,
As she fled.
The snouted satyrs drink clouted cream
'Neath the chestnut-trees as thick as a dream;
So I went,
And leant,
Where none but the doltish coltish wind

Nuzzled my hand for what it could find.
As it neighed,
I said,
"Don't touch me, sir, don't touch me, I say,
You'll tumble my strawberries into the hay."
Those snow-mounds of silver that bee, the spring,
Has sucked his sweetness from, I will bring
With fair-haired plants and with apples chill
For the great god Pan's high altar . . . I'll spill
Not one!
So, in fun,
We rolled on the grass and began to run,
Chasing that gaudy satyr the Sun;
Over the haycocks, away we ran,
Crying, "Here be berries as sunburnt as Pan!"
But Silenus
Has seen us. . . .
He runs like the rough satyr Sun.

Come away!

Katherine Mansfield

Katherine Mansfield

(1888–1923)

Admired during her lifetime as much for her bohemian lifestyle as for her witty writing, Kathleen Mansfield Beauchamp was "born with good nerve, [for] she had learned comprehensive courage, and in a hard school," according to contemporary writer Elizabeth Bowen. Mansfield, one of New Zealand's most beloved novelists, was born in Wellington, the third of six children, and grew up in the country. As a teenager she was sent to London to study at Queen's College, and though she went back to New Zealand briefly, European intellectual life proved too seductive to abandon. She returned to the Continent, where she married George Bowden. After just one day of wedlock, Mansfield—by most accounts a woman of exceptional physical beauty, given to wildly romantic notions—left Bowden to go on tour with a musical entertainment troupe.

Growing up, Mansfield always kept a journal, but her first published collection of stories was written in Germany, where she had gone to recuperate from a miscarriage after leaving the stage. She also published pieces in the Theosophical Society's journal, *The New Age*, and in *Rhythm*, a periodical edited by Thomas Middleton Murry, with whom she began a passionate affair. Through him Mansfield met Virginia Woolf, D.H. Lawrence, and other influential writers. She and Murry lived for several years in Italy, Switzerland, and France before marrying in 1918. She adopted the pen name Katherine Mansfield as her writing career blossomed.

There is no typical Mansfield story. Her works range from great scenic sagas about New Zealand to sympathetic portrayals of the elderly to the sort of short, stylish pieces that presaged the modernist movement in fiction. Praised for her ability to identify telling details, Mansfield was a decided minimalist whose zeal for storytelling was never submerged in gimmicky writing. She was, however, considered bold for taking certain risks with her work. The short story "The Tiredness of Rosabel" uses the device, highly unusual for its time, of focusing not on the eponymous young woman's life, but rather on her daydream. Mansfield wrote several other stories highlighting the figments of her characters' imaginations.

Mansfield wrote eighty-eight stories, leaving more than a quarter of them unfinished. In her twenties, she fell ill with venereal disease, which went untreated, and also contracted tuberculosis. The combination of these afflictions led to her untimely demise at the age of thirty-four, at Fontainebleau, outside Paris. Some say that her death, by coming so early, left her work still at the experimental stage. "Bliss," from the volume *Bliss and Other Stories* (1921), is regarded as a Mansfield masterpiece and was inspired by a real dream with a happy-ending sensibility: "Oh, why did she feel so tender towards the whole world tonight? Everything was good—was right. All that happened seemed to fill again her brimming cup of bliss."

Mansfield's stories were collected in *The Short Stories of Katherine Mansfield* (1937). Her journals were also published posthumously, after being edited by Murry.

A grandmother's love for her granddaughter, and the granddaughter's startling realization of the finality of death, are poignantly described in this excerpt from the short story "At the Bay." Here, the smallest details of a New Zealand family's seaside holiday take on momentous proportions.

The green blinds were drawn in the bungalows of the summer colony. Over the verandahs, prone on the paddock, flung over the fences, there were exhausted-looking bathing-dresses and rough striped towels. Each back window seemed to have a pair of sand-shoes on the sill and some lumps of rock or a bucket or a collection of pawa shells. The bush quivered in a haze of heat; the sandy road was empty except for the Trouts' dog Snooker, who lay stretched in the very middle of it. His blue eye was turned up, his legs stuck out stiffly, and he gave an occasional desperate-sounding puff, as much as to say he had decided to make an end of it and was only waiting for some kind cart to come along.

"What are you looking at, my grandma" Why do you keep stopping and sort of staring at the wall?"

Kezia and her grandmother were taking their siesta together. The little girl, wearing only her short drawers and her underbodice, her arms and legs bare, lay on one of the puffed-up pillows of her grandma's bed, and the old woman, in a white ruffled dressing-gown, sat in a rocker at the window, with a long piece of pink knitting in her lap. This room that they shared, like the other rooms of the bungalow, was of light varnished wood and the floor was bare. The furniture was of the shabbiest, the simplest. The dressing table, for instance, was a packing-case in a sprigged muslin petticoat, and the mirror above was very strange; it was as though a little piece of forked lightning was imprisoned in it. On the table there stood a jar of sea-pinks, pressed so tightly together they looked more like a velvet pincushion, and a special shell which Kezia had given her grandma for a pin-tray, and another even more special which she had thought would make a very nice place for a watch to curl up in.

"Tell me, grandma," said Kezia.

The old woman sighed, whipped the wool twice round her thumb, and drew the bone needle through. She was casting on.

"I was thinking of your Uncle William, darling," she said quietly.

My Australian Uncle William?" said Kezia. She had another.

"Yes, of course."

"The one I never saw?"

"That was the one."

"Well, what happened to him?" Kezia knew perfectly well, but she wanted to be told again.

"He went to the mines, and he got a sunstroke there and died," said old Mrs. Fairfield.

Kezia blinked and considered the picture again . . . a little man fallen over like a tin soldier by the side of a big black hole.

"Does it make you sad to think about him, grandma?" She hated her grandma to be sad.

It was the old woman's turn to consider. Did it make her sad? To look back, back. To stare down the years, as Kezia had seen her doing. To look after *them*

as a woman does, long after *they* were out of sight. Did it make her sad? No, life was like that.

"No, Kezia."

"But why?" asked Kezia. She lifted one bare arm and began to draw things in the air. "Why did Uncle William have to die? He wasn't old."

Mrs. Fairfield began counting the stitches in threes. "It just happened," she said in an absorbed voice.

"Does everybody have to die?" asked Kezia.

"Everybody!"

"*Me?*" Kezia sounded fearfully incredulous.

"Some day, my darling."

"But grandma." Kezia waved her left leg and waggled the toes. They felt sandy. "What if I just won't?"

The old woman sighed again and drew a long thread from the ball.

"We're not asked, Kezia," she said sadly. "It happens to all of us sooner or later."

Kezia lay still thinking this over. She didn't want to die. It meant she would have to leave here, leave everywhere, for ever, leave—leave her grandma. She rolled over quickly.

"Grandma," she said in a startled voice.

"What, my pet!"

"*You're* not to die." Kezia was very decided.

"Ah, Kezia"—her grandma looked up and smiled and shook her head—"don't let's talk about it."

"But you're not to. You couldn't leave me. You couldn't not be there." This was awful. "Promise me you won't ever do it, grandma," pleaded Kezia.

The old woman went on knitting.

"Promise me! Say never!"

But still her grandma was silent.

Kezia rolled off the bed; she couldn't bear it any longer, and lightly she leapt on to her grandma's knees, clasped her hands round the old woman's throat and began kissing her, under the chin, behind the ear, and blowing down her neck.

"Say never . . . say never . . . say never—" She gasped between the kisses. And then she began, very softly and lightly, to tickle her grandma.

"Kezia!" The old woman dropped her knitting. She swung back in the rocker. She began to tickle Kezia. "Say never, say never, say never," gurgled Kezia, while they lay there laughing in each other's arms. "Come, that's enough, my squirrel! That's enough, my wild pony!" said old Mrs. Fairfield, setting her cap straight. "Pick up my knitting."

Both of them had forgotten what the "never" was about.

Zora Neale Hurston

(1901–1960)

"*I* love myself when I am laughing . . . and then again when I am looking mean and impressive," wrote Zora Neale Hurston to photographer Carl Van Vechten in 1934. She was referring to a series of pictures he had taken of her, but the line resonated and became the title of a seminal anthology of her work, which included fiction, essays, articles, autobiography, folklore, and journalism.

Hurston was born in Notasulga, Alabama, in 1901, though some sources claim that her birth date was actually 1891. Indeed, the stone marker placed on her grave in 1973 by writer Alice Walker reads, in part, "Zora Neale Hurston / 'A Genius of the South' / 1901[sic]–1960." What is indisputable is that between 1920 and 1950, she was America's most prolific black female writer, and one of its best observers of the way black people lived in the generation after slavery.

Hurston's family moved to Eatonville, Florida, an all-black community where her father was elected mayor. Her mother, who had encouraged her daughter's free-spirited creativity, died before Zora reached her teens, and her father soon remarried. At odds with her stepmother, she lived with various family members, then ran away with a traveling theater company. She finished high school in Baltimore, and enrolled in Howard University in Washington, D.C. To supplement grants and scholarships, she worked as a manicurist and domestic while attending college.

Hurston began publishing short stories in literary magazines, and won second prize in a writing contest. She moved to New York City to study anthropology at Barnard College. There, she developed an interest in black folklore, and accepted an assignment to

Zora Neale Hurston

record such tales from the American south. Sponsored by a wealthy arts patron, Zora drove through Louisiana, Mississippi, Florida, and Alabama, encouraging people to recount stories about ghosts, devils, witches, God, unexplainable events, and slavery. Those stories were published more than a decade later in *Mules and Men*, today regarded today as an important work of cultural anthropology.

In New York, Hurston became part of an exciting creative movement later known as the Harlem Renaissance, which celebrated African-American literature, music, and art as black southerners began moving north to the big cities. Witty and talented, she was one of its stars. During this fruitful period, she collaborated with Langston Hughes on *Mule Bone* (1930), a comic play based on black rural folk culture. Her first novel, *Jonah's Gourd Vine* (1934), drew heavily on her parents' life in Eatonville. She wrote *Their Eyes Were Watching God* (1937), generally regarded her finest book, in just seven weeks.

Despite her success, Hurston spent her final years inpoverty. She continued to write short stories and magazine articles, and worked as a maid, teacher, and librarian before her death in a welfare home in 1960. After a period of neglect, her work was rediscovered in the late 1960s.

At certain times I have no race, I am *me*. When I set my hat at a certain angle and saunter down Seventh Avenue, Harlem City, feeling as snooty as the lions in front of the Forty-Second Street Library, for instance. So far as my feelings are concerned, Peggy Hopkins Joyce on the Boule Mich with her gorgeous raiment, stately carriage, knees knocking together in a most aristocratic manner, has nothing on me. The cosmic Zora emerges. I belong to no race nor time. I am the eternal feminine with its string of beads.

I have no separate feeling about being an American citizen and colored. I am merely a fragment of the Great Soul that surges within the boundaries. My country, right or wrong.

Sometimes, I feel discriminated against, but it does not make me angry. It merely astonishes me. How can any deny themselves the pleasure of my company? It's beyond me.

But in the main, I feel like a brown bag of miscellany propped against a wall. Against a wall in company with other bags, white, red and yellow. Pour out the contents, and there is discovered a jumble of small things priceless and worthless. A first-water diamond, an empty spool, bits of broken glass, lengths of string, a key to a door long since crumbled away, a rusty knife-blade, old shoes saved for a road that never was and never will be, a nail bent under the weight of things too heavy for any nail, a dried flower or two still a little fragrant. In your hand is the brown bag. On the ground before you is the jumble it held— so much like the jumble in the bags, could they be emptied, that all might be dumped in a single heap and the bags refilled without altering the content of any greatly. A bit of colored glass more or less would not matter. Perhaps that is how the Great Stuffer of Bags filled them in the first place—who knows?

When Joe Starks, a "citified, stylish dressed man" came into her life, Janie Crawford hoped for happiness at last. But their marriage proved to be a profound disappointment. In Their Eyes Were Watching God, *the worldly, well-educated Hurston writes in the regional patois of the American South.*

Ah knows uh few things, and womenfolks thinks sometimes too!"

"Aw naw they don't. They just think they's thinkin'. When Ah see one thing Ah undestands ten. You see ten things and don't understand one."

Times and scenes like that put Janie to thinking about the inside state of her marriage. Time came when she fought back with her tongue as best she could, but it didn't do her any good. It just made Joe do more. He wanted her submission and he'd keep on fighting until he felt he had it.

So gradually, she pressed her teeth together and learned how to hush. The spirit of the marriage left the bedroom and took to living in the parlor. It was there to shake hands whenever company came to visit, but it never went back inside the bedroom again. So she put something in there to represent the spirit like a Virgin Mary image in a church. The bed was no longer a daisy-field for her and Joe to play in. It was a place where she went and laid down when she was sleepy and tired.

She wasn't petal-open anymore with him. She was twenty-four and seven years married when she knew. She found that out one day when he slapped her face in the kitchen. It happened over one of those dinners that chasten all women sometimes. They plan and they fix and they do, and then some kitchen-dwelling fiend slips a scrochy, soggy, tasteless mess into their pots and pans. Janie was a good cook, and Joe had looked forward to his dinner as a refuge from other things. So when the bread didn't rise and the fish wasn't quite done at the bone, and the rice was scorched, he slapped Janie until she had a ringing sound in her ears and told her about her brains before he stalked on back to the store.

Janie stood where he left her for unmeasured time and thought. She stood there until something fell off the shelf inside her. Then she went inside there to see what it was. It was her image of Jody tumbled down and shattered. But looking at it she saw that it never was the flesh and blood figure of her dreams. Just something she had grabbed up to drape her dreams over. In a way she turned her back upon the image where it lay and looked further. She had no more blossomy openings dusting pollen over her man, neither any glistening young fruit where the petals used to be. She found that she had a host of thoughts she had never expressed to him, and numerous emotions she had never let Jody know about. Things packed up and put away in parts of her heart where he could never find them. She was saving up feelings for some man she had never seen. She had an inside and an outside now and suddenly she knew how not to mix them.

Jean Rhys

(1894–1979)

Creating unforgettable female characters—most of them elegant, jaded, possessed of fading glamour, and poised to relinquish their search for a better life—was the specialty of Jean Rhys. These shabby-souled women evoke a certain "There but for the grace of God go I" feeling that speaks eloquently to many contemporary readers.

Jean Rhys was born in Dominica, the West Indies, the daughter of a Welsh doctor and a Creole (white West Indian) mother. Memories of her childhood on the tropical island, with its dramatic secrets and rituals, influenced her work in later years. At sixteen she moved to London, where she married a Dutch poet. They roved through Europe in the Twenties as partners in wanderlust, ending up in Paris. There Rhys met the British novelist and poet Ford Madox Ford, who encouraged her to write.

Rhys's life thus far had been colorful, and she captured some of its essence in her first book, a collection of stories called *The Left Bank* (1927), set in the seedy-but-charming Montparnasse cafes and hotels she frequented. In its preface, Ford praised "the singular instinct for form possessed by this young lady, an instinct for form being possessed by singularly few writers of English and by almost no English women writers."

An unappealing character who may have been modeled on Ford appeared in Rhys's next book, *Quartet* (1928). This novel recounts the eerie *ménage à trois* between a wealthy, imperious German man, his long-suffering wife, and Marya, a young woman whose husband is in prison. Following the publication of *After Leaving Mr. Mackenzie* (1930), the deliciously depressing saga of a mistress whose lover cuts off her financial support, Rhys returned to England. There she wrote *Voyage in the Dark* (1934), about a dreamy-eyed young woman who grows up in the Caribbean, moves to England, has her heart broken by a faithless lover, and

Jean Rhys

becomes a prostitute. In *Good Morning, Midnight* (1939), the protagonist, Sasha, is a fortyish woman who regrets her lost youth, drinks too much, and pursues the wrong man.

Rhys moved to Cornwall after the publication of *Good Morning, Midnight,* and her five books went out of print. She didn't surface until 1958, when an adaptation of her last novel was broadcast on British radio. During her hiatus, she had written a number of stories, later collected in *Tigers Are Better-Looking* (1968) and *Sleep It Off, Lady* (1976). She had also been at work on a novel which many critics feel is her finest. In *Wide Sargasso Sea* (1966), Rhys weaves a mesmerizing fictional account of the life of Mrs. Rochester, the mad first wife in Charlotte Brontë's *Jane Eyre.* She imagines the woman—unlike other Rhys characters, a true heroine—as a Creole heiress who enjoys an idyllic childhood in Dominica and Jamaica. Then the mysterious Mr. Rochester appears and takes her away to England, where everything changes. As in Rhys's other stories, there is no happy ending. But for the author herself, *Wide Sargasso Sea* renewed interest in her other works, which were reprinted and are enjoyed around the world today.

In this excerpt from Wide Sargasso Sea, *Rhys writes in the voice of Mr. Rochester, the enigmatic aristocrat who travels to Jamaica and meets the woman who will become his wife. (As readers of Charlotte Brontë's* Jane Eyre *know, her lot is not destined to be a happy one.) Here Rochester revels in the exotic mysteries of Caribbean life, totally beguiled by the lovely young woman he is about to marry.*

I woke to the sound of voices in the next room, laughter and water being poured out. I listened, still drowsy. Antoinette said, "Don't put any more scent on my hair. He doesn't like it." The other: "The man don't like scent? I never hear that before." It was almost dark.

The dining-room was brilliantly lit. Candles on the table, a row on the sideboard, three-branch candlesticks on the old sea-chest. The two doors on to the veranda stood open but there was no wind. The flames burned straight. She was sitting on the sofa and I wondered why I had never realized how beautiful she was. Her hair was combed away from her face and fell smoothly far below her waist. I could see the red and gold lights in it. She seemed pleased when I complimented her on her dress and told me she had it made in St. Pierre, Martinique. "They call this fashion *à la Joséphine.*"

"You talk of St. Pierre as though it were Paris," I said.

"But it is the Paris of the West Indies."

There were trailing pink flowers on the table and the name echoed pleasantly in my head. Coralita Coralita. The food, though too highly seasoned, was lighter and more appetizing than anything I had tasted in Jamaica. We drank champagne. A great many moths and beetles found their way into the room, flew into the candles and fell dead on the tablecloth. Amélie swept them up with a crumb brush. Uselessly. More moths and beetles came.

"Is it true," she said, "that England is like a dream? Because one of my friends who married an Englishman wrote and told me so. She said this place London is like a cold dark dream sometimes. I want to wake up."

"Well," I answered annoyed, "that is precisely how your beautiful island seems to me, quite unreal and like a dream."

"But how can rivers and mountains and the sea be unreal?"

"And how can millions of people, their houses and their streets be unreal?"

"More easily," she said, "much more easily. Yes a big city must be like a dream."

"No, this is unreal and like a dream," I thought.

The long veranda was furnished with canvas chairs, two hammocks, and a wooden table on which stood a tripod telescope. Amélie brought out candles with glass shades but the night swallowed up the feeble light. There was a very strong scent of flowers—the flowers by the river that open at night she told me—and the noise, subdued in the inner room, was deafening. "Crac-cracs," she explained, "they make a sound like their name, and crickets and frogs."

I leaned on the railing and saw hundreds of fireflies—"Ah yes, fireflies in Jamaica, here they call a firefly La belle."

A large moth, so large that I thought it was a bird, blundered into one of the candles, put it out and fell to the floor. "He's a big fellow," I said.

"Is it badly burned?"

"More stunned than hurt."

I took the beautiful creature up in my hand-kerchief and put it on the railing. For a moment it was still and by the dim candlelight I could see the soft brilliant colours, the intricate pattern on the wings. I shook the handkerchief gently and it flew away.

"I hope that gay gentleman will be safe," I said.

"He will come back if we don't put the candles out. It's light enough by the stars."

Indeed the starlight was so bright that shadows of the veranda posts and the trees outside lay on the floor.

"Now come for a walk," she said, "and I will tell you a story."

We walked along the veranda to the steps which led to the lawn.

"We used to come here to get away from the hot weather in June, July and August. I came three times with my Aunt Cora who is ill. That was after . . ." She stopped and put her hand up to her head.

"If this is a sad story, don't tell it to me tonight."

"It is not sad," she said. "Only some things happen and are there for always even though you forget why or when. It was in that little bedroom."

I looked where she was pointing but could only see the outline of a narrow bed and one or two chairs.

"This night I can remember it was very hot. The window was shut but I asked Christophine to open it because the breeze comes from the hills at night. The land breeze. Not from the sea. It was so hot that my night chemise was sticking to me but I went to sleep all the same. And then suddenly I was awake. I saw two enormous rats, as big as cats, on the sill staring at me."

"I'm not astonished that you were frightened."

"But I was not frightened. That was the strange thing. I stared at them and they did not move. I could see myself in the looking-glass the other side of the room, in my white chemise with a frill round the neck, staring at those rats and the rats quite still, staring at me."

"Well, what happened?"

"I turned over, pulled up the sheet and went to sleep instantly."

"And is that the story?"

"No, I woke up again suddenly like the first time and the rats were not there but I felt very frightened. I got out of bed quickly and ran on to the veranda. I lay down in this hammock. This one." She pointed to a flat hammock, a rope at each of the four corners.

"There was a full moon that night—and I watched it for a long time. There were no clouds chasing it, so it seemed to be standing still and it shone on me. Next morning Christophine was angry. She said that it was very bad to sleep in the moonlight when the moon is full."

"And did you tell her about the rats?"

"No, I never told anyone till now. But I have never forgotten them."

I wanted to say something reassuring but the scent of the river flowers was overpoweringly strong. I felt giddy.

"Do you think that too," she said, "that I have slept too long in the moonlight?"

Vita Sackville-West

(1892–1962)

A prolific English novelist, poet, reporter and biographer, Victoria Mary Sackville-West wrote about her childhood in *The Edwardians* (1930), set at the family estate of Knole. She was born the aristocratic daughter of Baron Sackville and was privately educated. Sackville-West's life changed significantly for the first time in 1914, when she wed Harold Nicolson, a public servant, and began their marriage by accompanying him on overseas postings with the British Legation. She found travel an exhilarating experience and developed an extreme consciousness of "place," whether it was a foreign marketplace or a stately home in the British countryside.

After a few years, Vita grew tired of following her husband and chose to remain in England, finding romantic and intellectual companionship with women while he was away. In 1918 she "eloped" with the British novelist Violet Trefusis, a liaison that lasted until 1921. Her intimate friendship with Virginia Woolf inspired Woolf's *Orlando*, and the two remained friends for years.

One of her earliest works, *Knole and the Sackvilles* (1922), bespeaks Sackville-West's dejection at being unable to inherit her family's estate because of her gender. The same year, she wrote the novel *Heritage*, which describes her preoccupation with how patrimony affects genetics. The spring of 1926 found Vita, smartly dressed and laden with Vuitton trunks, traveling to Persia by way of India and Egypt, and returning home via Russia. Along the way she chronicled her adventures with photographs and journal entries, both published in *Passenger to Teheran* later that year. In a different vein, she wrote a long pastoral poem, *The Land* (1927). Despite Nicolson's own homosexuality and her affairs, the couple had a son, Nigel (who grew up to be a writer himself, documenting his parents' unorthodox life together in *Portrait of a Marriage*, published in 1973).

In 1930, Vita began a novel with a decidedly feminist point of view about independent widowhood and the way property is affected by patrimony. Called *All Passion Spent*, it was published the following year. Meanwhile, Sackville-West and her husband took up residence in the crumbling ruins of Sissinghurst Castle, a seventeenth-century relic, and she worked feverishly to restore the grounds. Finally, she had an ancestral home to call her own. She and Nicolson both became passionate about horticulture. The world they created has become one of England's most distinguished private gardens. She drew on the experience for inspiration as she wrote the long poem *Sissinghurst* (1931) and the book *English Country Homes* (1942).

Vita Sackville-West received the most public acclaim, and the most money, for her elegantly written novels. But she also continued to write poetry and pursued an interest in women's roles in the spiritual world. The results of the latter are the biography *Saint Joan of Arc* (1936) and a study of two female saints, Teresa of Avila and Thérèse of Lisieux, called *The Eagle and the Dove* (1943). Sackville-West's letters have been published in two volumes.

In these excerpts from Passenger to Teheran, *the restless British aristocrat documents her journey to Persia, where her husband has preceded her on diplomatic business. Sackville-West employs her characteristically mesmerizing language to evoke all she sees.*

This country through which I have been hurled for four days has become stationary at last; instead of rushing past me, it has slowed down and finally stopped; the hills stand still, they allow me to observe them; I no longer catch but a passing glimpse of them in a certain light, but may watch their changes during any hour of the day; I may walk over them and see their stones lying quiet, may become acquainted with the small life of their insects and lichens; I am no longer a traveller, but an inhabitant. I have my own house, dogs, and servants; my luggage has at last been unpacked. The ice-box is in the kitchen, the gramophone on the table, and my books are on the shelves. It is spring; long avenues of judas trees have come into flower along the roads, the valleys are full of peach-blossom, the snow is beginning to melt on the Elburz. The air, at this altitude of nearly four thousand feet, is as pure as the note of a violin. There is everywhere a sense of openness and of being at a great height; that sense of grime and over-population, never wholly absent in European countries, is wholly absent here; it is like being lifted up and set above the world on a great, wide roof—the plateau of Iran. . . .

Perched up on their scaffolding in a dark whitewashed barn of the bazaars, the carpet-makers threaded their spindles, sitting with dangling legs twenty feet above ground before the stretched warp and woof of the carpet. They sat in a row, as swallows on a telegraph wire, ten or twelve of them, weaving

Vita Sackville-West

with the quick hands of practice. Little boys in round cashmere caps, young men in blue linen, they presented a row of backs, and of crossed feet swinging in long, pointed, white canvas shoes, and as they wove they chattered, pulling at the coloured wools, knocking the stitches down into place, leaning forward, reaching for another skein. As the eyes grew accustomed to the darkness, the rich texture of the carpet emerged in blues and reds; like a half-lived life, stretched on its frame, the pattern of the lower half was clear, but the upper half still rose naked, the brown strings waiting for the daily inch of the design. Shafts of sunlight speared the room, shooting down from holes in the roof, and quivering in circles on the floor. In a corner stood a great wooden framework, a rude primitive contrivance of stays, rollers, and pulleys, laced with twine; squatting in front of this, three women, veritable Parcae, spun the wool on to distaffs. The heavy woollen skeins hung like clusters of fruit; as red as pomegranates, as blue as grapes, as yellow as lemons; they jumped and bobbed with the spinning; the roughened fingers ran up and down the drawn-out strands, robbing them of their beard, before the quick twist spun them up into the conical ball on the distaff. The women looked up with a grin: here was something that they could do better than the superior foreigner. All their lives (I supposed) they had known, day in, day out, this rasp of the wool between their fingers, until, for them, it became the one physical sensation intimately known; the one habitual thing that would trudge through their half-dreams between sleeping and waking. But they were unaware that I supposed this; nor, being aware, would they have cared or understood, any more than the Egyptian potters, for life is rough and practical, and there is no time for those finer shades that delight the idle. An unchanged, traditional industry; that rude barn enshrined all the quality of the ancient crafts, in essence the same as the carpenter's shop, the forge, the wine-press; full of the clumsy laborious processes of such immemorial trades, but rich in a spirit denied to the apter methods of convenience. The art of carpet-making is not dead in Persia. Not only does it thrive in Isfahan, but in the tents of the nomad tribes the women weave, according to the traditional pattern of their province; they weave for their own use, and for the markets, keeping the hereditary skill alive, on the hillside and by the fires. How many people, in England, look intelligently at the rug they trample? How many people, who peer into a picture or examine a chair, will bring an equal fastidiousness to bear upon a carpet? Yet a carpet is a work of art with a special chance of appealing to even the most general taste; it is no otiose ornament, but a necessity, and furthermore, by its symmetry of design it panders to the human predilection for a repeated pattern. It can share either the flat quality of fresco, or the deep opulence of texture. For all that, it is neglected save by a few, and even by those few it is liable to be maltreated and hung upon a wall, which is not the proper place for a carpet.

Edna St. Vincent Millay

(1892–1950)

"Vincent," as she was known to her family, was petite with wavy red-gold hair. The oldest of three sisters, she was born in Rockland, Maine. Her father was a teacher who had risen to the position of superintendent of schools, and her mother wrote and played music until the couple divorced, when she took a job as a practical nurse to support her children. From her, Edna learned to play piano and write poems, which were published in the St. *Nicholas* magazine for children. She went on to edit her high school literary magazine.

A national prize for a poem called "Renascence" earned Edna enough acclaim that admirers of her talent helped arrange for her a much-needed scholarship to college. At Vassar and then at Barnard, she continued to win poetry prizes. After graduation in 1917, she moved to Greenwich Village and published her first book, *Renascence and Other Poems*.

Millay supported herself by writing short stories, translating songs, and working as an actress, director, and playwright for the Provincetown Players. She traveled to Europe on an assignment from *Vanity Fair* in 1921 and lived abroad for several years—for a while, with her mother, though she also struck out on adventurous horseback treks. She returned to the U.S. to great acclaim over the publication of three books: *A Few Figs from Thistles* (1920), *Second April* (1921), and *Aria da Capo* (1920). Critics noted her unconventional celebration of womanhood, the antiwar sentiments she so candidly expressed, and her rebellious feminist soul, portrayed in such lyrics as this from the poem "Departure":

Precocious as always, Millay won the Pulitzer Prize in 1922, at the age of 30. A year later she married Eugen Boissevain, a Dutch importer who was the widower of the feminist Inez Mulholland, and spent the next year traveling the world with him. In 1925 they moved to a country retreat on eight hundred acres in the Berkshires of upstate New York, though he

Edna St. Vincent Millay

accompanied her on frequent reading tours around the country. She also read her poetry on Sunday night radio programs and wrote the libretto for *The King's Henchman* (1927), which was produced at the Metropolitan Opera House.

Shortly before World War II broke out, Millay suffered a back injury which was to plague her for years. She contributed to the war effort by writing speeches, radio shows, and poetry to the point of nervous exhaustion. Afterwards, she and Boissevain remained at their farm while she continued to write. After his death she remained there alone and died a year later, early in the morning, after working on her poetry all night long.

A tribute of such quietly powerful beauty to rival Elizabeth Barrett Browning's Sonnets *from the Portuguese, Millay's poem "Love Is Not All" (1931) concerns the resolute certainty of love. In a lighter vein, she celebrates a woman who would just as soon let the housework go undone while she enjoys nature in "Portrait by a Neighbour" (1931).*

[Love Is Not All]

Love is not all: it is not meat nor drink
Nor slumber nor a roof against the rain;
Nor yet a floating spar to men that sink
And rise and sink and rise and sink again;
Love can not fill the thickened lung with breath,
Nor clean the blood, nor set the fractured bone;
Yet many a man is making friends with death
Even as I speak, for lack of love alone.
It well may be that in a difficult hour,
Pinned down by pain and moaning for release,
Or nagged by want past resolution's power,
I might be driven to sell your love for peace,
Or trade the memory of this night for food.
It well may be. I do not think I would.

Portrait by a Neighbour

Before she has her floor swept
    Or her dishes done,
Any day you'll find her
    A-sunning in the sun!

It's long after midnight
    Her key's in the lock,
And you never see her chimney smoke
    Till past ten o'clock!

She digs in her garden
    With a shovel and a spoon,
She weeds her lazy lettuce
    By the light of the moon,

She walks up the walk
    Like a woman in a dream,
She forgets she borrowed butter
    And pays you back cream!

Her lawn looks like a meadow,
    And if she mows the place
She leaves the clover standing
    And the Queen Anne's lace!

Dorothy Parker

(1893–1967)

"**M**rs. Parker had been a writer whose robust and acid lucidities had been much feared and admired," wrote *New Yorker* critic Brendan Gill in the introduction to her collected works. Indeed, rapier-edged wisecracks and painful realism are the hallmarks of Dorothy Parker's art. Her prodigious output of short stories and poetry, set against a background of the "fast life" in early twentieth-century Manhattan, is characterized by a flippant, ironic attitude toward depression, alcoholism, and relationships between men and women.

Dorothy Rothschild was born in West End, New Jersey, to a Jewish father and a Scottish mother. Her mother died less than a year later. Dorothy would later mine the misery of her adolescence, spent with a despised stepmother and her uncaring father, in numerous poems and stories. After graduating from a private school in New Jersey, she found a job at *Vogue*, writing captions for fashion layouts. Soon she moved to another Conde Nast publication, *Vanity Fair*, where she was made drama critic. In her mid-twenties, she married a man named Edward Pond Parker II, from whom she was divorced several years later. She continued to use his name, which she preferred to her own.

For Parker, the Roaring Twenties were loud indeed. She lived a reckless, turbulent life, drinking excessively and often contemplating suicide. "What fresh hell is this?" she wondered in one famous poem. In another sad, witty rumination about the various distasteful ways to take one's own life, she concluded that, after all, "You might as well live." When her poems were first published, critics panned them as frivolous little ditties.

That changed when one of Parker's stories appeared in *The New Yorker*. She became a frequent presence in that distinguished literary magazine, contributing short stories and book reviews as its "Constant Reader." Her first poetry volume, *Enough Rope* (1926),

Dorothy Parker

allowed her to quit her regular *Vanity Fair* job and write full time. She also became the most famous female member of the Algonquin Round Table, a gathering of noted writers who congregated at the midtown Manhattan hotel in the early Thirties. Among her literary drinking cronies were Ernest Hemingway, Ring Lardner, and William Faulkner.

In the mid-1930s, Parker married again, this time to Alan Campbell, an actor-screenwriter with whom she collaborated on the 1937 script for *A Star Is Born*. The marriage was often rocky. Parker and Campbell divorced, remarried, separated, and then lived together until his death in 1963.

During the McCarthy era, Parker was blacklisted in Hollywood as a Communist supporter and found it difficult to get work. Her last project was a play called *The Ladies of the Corridor* (1964), about a group of lonely widows living in a residential hotel. The play closed after forty-five performances and bad reviews. When she died, Parker left her estate to civil rights leader the Rev. Martin Luther King, Jr.

Parker was known primarily for her acid wit and sharp tongue, but as shown in this excerpt from a short story entitled "The Lovely Leave," she also understood how difficult it can be to maintain one's mental equilibrium when afflicted with the acute pains of love and longing.

Her husband had telephoned her by long distance to tell her about the leave. She had not expected the call, and she had no words arranged. She threw away whole seconds explaining her surprise at hearing him, and reporting that it was raining hard in New York, and asking was it terribly hot where he was. He had stopped her to say, look, he didn't have time to talk long; and he had told her quickly that his squadron was to be moved to another field the next week and on the way he would have twenty-four hours' leave. It was difficult for her to hear. Behind his voice came a jagged chorus of young male voices, all crying the syllable "Hey!"

"Ah, don't hang up yet," she said. "Please. Let's talk another minute, just another———"

"Honey, I've got to go," he said. "The boys all want a crack at the telephone. See you a week from today, around five. 'By."

Then there had been a click as his receiver went back into place. Slowly she cradled her telephone, looking at it as if all frustrations and bewilderments and separations were its fault. Over it she had heard his voice, coming from far away. All the months, she had tried not to think of the great blank distance between them; and now that far voice made her know she had thought of nothing else. And his speech had been brisk and busy. And from back of him had come gay, wild young voices, voices he heard every day and she did not, voices of those who shared his new life. And he had heeded them and not her, when she begged for another minute. She took her hand off the telephone and held it away from her with fingers spread stiffly apart, as if it had touched something horrid.

Then she told herself to stop her nonsense. If you looked for things to make you feel hurt and wretched and unnecessary, you were certain to find them, more easily each time, so easily, soon, that you did not even realize you had gone out searching. Women alone often developed into experts at the practice. She must never join their dismal league.

What was she dreary about, anyway? If he had only a little while to talk, then he had only a little while to talk, that was all. Certainly he had had time to tell her he was coming, to say that they would be together soon. And there she was, sitting scowling at the telephone, the kind, faithful telephone that had brought her the lovely news. She would see him in a week. Only a week. She began to feel, along her back and through her middle, little quivers of excitement, like tiny springs uncoiling into spirals.

There must be no waste to this leave. She thought of the preposterous shyness that had fallen upon her when he had come home before. It was the first time she had seen him in uniform. There he stood, in their little apartment, a dashing stranger in strange, dashing garments. Until he had gone into the army, they had never spent a night apart in all their marriage; and when she saw him, she dropped her eyes and twisted her handkerchief and could bring nothing but monosyllables from her throat. There must be no such squandering of minutes this time. There must be no such gangling diffidence to lop even an instant from their twenty-four hours of perfect union. Oh, Lord, only twenty-four hours. . . .

No. That was exactly the wrong thing to do; that was directly the wrong way to think. That was the way she had spoiled it before. Almost as soon as the shyness had left her and she felt she knew him again, she had begun counting. She was so filled with the desperate consciousness of the hours sliding away—only twelve more, only five, oh, dear God, only one left—that she had no room for gaiety and ease. She had spent the golden time in grudging its going.

She had been so woebegone of carriage, so sad and slow of word as the last hour went, that he, nervous under the pall, had spoken sharply and there had been a quarrel. When he had had to leave for his train, there were no clinging farewells, no tender words to keep. He had gone to the door and opened it and stood with it against his shoulder while he shook out his flight cap and put it on, adjusting it with great care, one inch over the eye, one inch above the ear. She stood in the middle of the living-room, cool and silent, looking at him.

When his cap was precisely as it should be, he looked at her.

"Well," he said. He cleared his throat. "Guess I'd better get going."

"I'm sure you had," she said.

He studied his watch intently. "I'll just make it," he said.

"I'm sure you will," she said.

She turned, not with an actual shrug, only with the effect of one, and went to the window and looked out, as if casually remarking the weather. She heard the door close loudly and then the grind of the elevator.

When she knew he was gone, she was cool and still no longer. She ran about the little flat, striking her breast and sobbing.

Then she had two months to ponder what had happened, to see how she had wrought the ugly small ruin. She cried in the nights.

She need not brood over it any more. She had her lesson; she could forget how she had learned it. This new leave would be the one to remember, the one he and she would have, to keep forever. She was to have a second chance, another twenty-four hours with him. After all, that is no short while, you know; that is, if you do not think of it as a thin little row of hours dropping off like beads from a broken string. Think of it as a whole long day and a whole long night, shining and sweet, and you will be all but awed by your fortune. For how many people are there who have the memory of a whole long day and a whole long night, shining and sweet, to carry with them in their hearts until they die?

Stevie Smith

(1902–1971)

"Who and what is Stevie Smith?/ Is she woman? Is she myth?" wrote Ogden Nash about the British poet on the occasion of the United States publication of her *Selected Poems* (1962). The enigmatic Smith appeared to the literary world as a rather eccentric figure who illustrated her work with odd doodles and made up her own rules about poetic form. On the face of it, her verse appears simplistic, as pared-down and small as the movements of her own life. However, like the works of Emily Dickinson, many of Smith's poems are fraught with muffled passion, sexual anxiety, and other distressing aspects of the human condition.

Born in Hull, Yorkshire, Florence Margaret Smith never knew her father. At the age of three, she moved with her mother and older sister to live with her aunt in Palmers Green, London. There she attended the North London Collegiate School for Girls, known for its progressive philosophy that boys and girls study the same well-rounded curriculum. Smith was devoted to her aunt, an irascible figure known as "Auntie Lion," and cared for her until the aunt's death. As a child she was nicknamed Stevie, after a famous jockey. Even as an adult, she remained diminutive.

After graduation, Smith took a secretarial job at Newnes and Pearson, a London magazine publishing firm. There she learned the business, benefiting from her education in finance to the point that she made numerous profitable investments. At the same typewriter where Smith handled her business correspondence, she worked at her writing. Her first book, *Novel on Yellow Paper* (1936) was published when she was thirty-three. Smith's anarchic device of intercutting prose with large segments of poetry captured the attention of critics, who deemed it on the literary cutting edge. She also spent two years on the editorial staff of the *Observer* magazine.

Stevie Smith

Smith never quite fit in. Or as she put it: "I was much too far out all my life/ And not waving but drowning." Suicide figures prominently in her work, and she weighed its possibilities matter-of-factly. *A Good Time Was Had by All* (1937), her first volume of poetry, was followed by two melancholy, understated novels—*The Holiday* (1949) and *Over the Frontier* (1938)—and the chilling volume of verse *Not Waving but Drowning* (1957). In addition to conducting poetry readings (sometimes, more like poetry chantings) in public and on the radio, Smith also wrote literary criticism and elegant, scathing nonfiction. One of her most critically acclaimed stories describes a private audience with Queen Elizabeth in 1969, before receiving the Queen's Medal for Poetry. Smith was always more popular in her native England than in the U.S., and it was only in the early 1980s that all of her novels became available in America. At that time, she was also, improbably, the subject of a film based on a play, both of them entitled *Stevie*. Pragmatism was Smith's specialty. "Come, Death," is the title of her last poem, composed shortly before she succumbed to a brain tumor at the age of sixty-nine.

"The Friend" (1938) is an encouraging tribute that acknowledges how wearying it can be to simply go through the motions of one's life. Language rich in recurring sounds imbues "Pretty" (1962), Smith's unflinching reappraisal of a word that can be quite ordinary, with great conviction.

The Friend

We needs must love the highest when we see it,
And having seen it knowing lower flee it.
But whither flee
Exiled from bliss
In these sad days
Of nothingness,
Shall we,
Trailing the tired wing of happier flights,
Hemmed in by lower presents mourn past heights,
And in a phrase
Of bitterness
Throw
All our woe?
No, gentle soul,

If fate and all the world have wronged thee,
And every spectre of despite has thronged thee,
Keep fast
Thy visionary past,
A part of present's whole
And but a part.
Thus happiness
And grief in thy stout heart
Shall range thee higher than th' angelic bands
Who know bliss but no smart
And serve
With happy but not midnight clenched hands
A lower place deserve.
But thou of present depth and former height
Has highest height attained and needst no flight.

Pretty

Why is the word pretty so underrated?
  In November the leaf is pretty when it falls
The stream grows deep in the woods after rain
And in the pretty pool the pike stalks

He stalks his prey, and this is pretty too,
The prey escapes with an underwater flash
But not for long, the great fish has him now
The pike is a fish who always has his prey

And this is pretty. The water rat is pretty
His paws are not webbed, he cannot shut his nostrils
As the otter can and the beaver, he is torn between
The land and water. Not 'torn', he does not mind.

The owl hunts in the evening and it is pretty
The lake water below him rustles with ice
There is frost coming from the ground, in the
     air mist
All this is pretty, it could not be prettier.

Yes, it could always be prettier, the eye abashes
It is becoming an eye that cannot see enough,
Out of the wood the eye climbs. This is prettier
A field in the evening, tilting up.

The field tilts to the sky. Though it is late
The sky is lighter than the hill field
All this looks easy but really it is extraordinary
Well, it is extraordinary to be so pretty.

And it is careless, and that is always pretty
This field, this owl, this pike, this pool are careless,
As Nature is always careless and indifferent
Who sees, who steps, means nothing, and this
     is pretty.

M.F.K. Fisher

M.F.K. Fisher

(1908–1992)

*A*nyone who enjoys reading about food cherishes the essays and stories of Mary Frances Kennedy Fisher. Her landmark work *The Art of Eating* (1954), an enormous tome mixing recipes, social commentary, travel writing, and romantic storytelling, has inspired decades of aspiring American chefs.

Born in Albion, Michigan, Fisher spent her childhood in Whittier, California. Her well-to-do parents enjoyed dining out and took her to many fine restaurants, detailed recollections of which were to enhance her later writings. She had a peripatetic academic life, attending the University of Illinois and U.C.L.A. before graduating from college in Dijon, France. Fisher's gastronomic education came when she translated *The Physiology of Taste* (1948), one of the most famous food treatises in history, written by the eighteenth-century French politician, magistrate, and gourmand Jean Anthelme Brillat-Savarin.

Coming of age in the years before World War II, Fisher had the opportunity to travel when living abroad was cheap and rewarding. With her first husband, Al Fisher, she explored the countryside of France. Returning to America during the Depression, Fisher fell in love with Dillwyn Parrish, a friend of her and her husband's. They married and moved to Switzerland, where they operated a vineyard for several years until Parrish was stricken with a rare disease and died. Fisher was left with two daughters, many friends, and an unquenchable zeal to keep traveling and writing.

An accomplished proponent of simple cooking and a strong believer in the nourishing aspects of both food and love (the latter, both maternal and sensual), Fisher published *Serve It Forth*, a collection of food essays, in 1937; *Consider the Oyster* in 1941; and *How to Cook a Wolf*, full of hints for humble eating pleasure in a wartime period of food rationing, in 1942. Later, all were collected with two other books into the hefty *The Art of Eating*.

Fisher could couch in sophisticated prose such useful culinary recommendations as soaking sliced raw onions in milk for an hour before adding them to salads, to make them taste mild and sweet. She could also adopt a curmudgeon's palate when writing about the crassness of some dishes beloved by Americans: "Who first served a Caesar or Cesar or even Cicero salad: (I know of at least two people who have been actively repelled by the headwaiter's ritual of breaking barely coddled eggs over this mishmash at the last minute, in posh restaurants. . . .)"

Though best known for her gastronomical works, Fisher also wrote with great poetic prowess and innate dignity about the pain and joy of motherhood and marriage. *A Considerable Town* (1980) described Marseille, where she once lived. *Sister Age* (1983) examined the process of growing old, and *Among Friends* (1990), her own California childhood. She spent the last years of her life in the wine country of northern California, first in St. Helena and then in Glen Ellen, in the Sonoma Valley. She died in her stucco-and-tile house while working on *Stay Me, Oh Comfort Me* (1993), her seventeenth book. Though it began with the ironic observation that, "I find increasingly as I grow older that I do not consider myself a writer," her legions of devoted readers would surely never concur.

In "Mrs. Teeters' Tomato Jar," Fisher celebrates the beauty of an ordinary object. Characteristically, it's an object from a kitchen.

The jar is made of clear hard glass, hand-blown into six sides but rounding at the top to a perfect open circle. It is about ten inches tall and five wide, at the bottom, and holds ten cups of anything. Probably there are others like it in collections of early American glass, but I'd wager that there is not one colored so delicately a subtle mauve, from lying under the desert sun between Indio and 29 Palms on the California sands. Except for the shadow of a bubble on one side, it is flawless. How did it last so long without a chip or crack or, more probable, complete shattering in a storm or any other violence?

I take good care of it, aware of its neat umbilicus left by the blower, and of its fine functional design that tapers from many-sided to round in one pure topping, and especially of its unattainable coloring. If it could have lain on the hot sand for another few decades it would surely have turned a deep purple, as good glass used to do. But then or even now it would have been bulldozed by a subdivision road-builder, or crushed by a dune buggy. . . .

A few days ago it looked especially beautiful, with a few late-blooming lilies in it. Their stems, paled through the lavender glass, were pearled with tiny gleaming bubbles. The long golden light of late September shone on one side of the vase and straight out the other. A friend exclaimed, "Oh, it's from Venice, from Venezia-Murano one hundred years ago! Where did you find it?" And without even thinking, I said, "Yes, that's Mrs. Teeters' tomato jar." And it was then that I realized that I am probably the only person in the whole world who now knows about Mrs. Teeters, and that I had better explain, while I can, a little about how her jar came into my hands.

(Everything in this report is either plain fact, hearsay, surmise, or wishful fantasy, a heady combination when there is nobody to say me nay! The jar is certainly a reality, and it was given to me by a real man named Arnold in about 1940.)

When my friend brought me the jar, he had filled it over many years with layers of colored sands, from flashing white to dark grey-browns and reds, all seen through the pale lavender of the sides. It weighed several pounds, and in a few years I emptied it onto yet another desert floor, and from then on it has held all kinds of weeds and flowers, and once some fine shells, but never cooked tomatoes.

Arnold was a reformed desert rat. Late in his life, he mended his lone wild ways for a round little woman and then their two little round daughters, but until Lina roped and tied him he was probably one of the last real "rats" to drift silently through Western lands where no sane person could survive. He and the other shadowy men, refugees from one form or another of imprisonment, lived then and perhaps still

do live in ways that the rest of us do not comprehend; like the bleached snakes and mice and spiders of the great deserts of this country, they know where to find matching shadows: a leaf, a rock. They know how to drink cactus-water, and one drop of dew, and above all when to let it touch their lips. They can survive for many days without swallowing. They become aloof and silent in the hottest months, and it is only at night that they emerge, like all the other creatures of their world.

As winter sets in, though, and the sun is kinder, they begin their walks toward legendary gold mines, hidden treasures cached by the conquistadores, veins of amethyst and opal. They walk endless miles, their worlds on their backs and in their dreams, and Arnold told me that although they don't talk much, in case they might let some clue slip about hidden booty only they must find, they like to rest and eat together.

One fall I was sitting in a hamburger joint with Arnold, in Indio where we went to buy dates, and two strangely faded men with wrinkled faces and pale eyes stood looking through the window, plainly communicating with him but without moving more than a few muscles. I asked him if they would come in for coffee, and he said, "Not on your life! That's two buddies of mine. They're on their way out, with supplies. I may see them next spring, if they make it." I said they looked like sand, only browner, and he said, "We kind of dry up. But when we can, we sure *eat!* It never shows."

And it seems, from what Arnold told me over

many more seasons, that there once was a Mrs. Teeters who knew most of these wordless desert ghosts, and fed them. That was why he brought me her tomato jar, he said: we were both good handy women at the stove.

(From now on, having settled that there was this woman and that she did leave one beautiful jar lying on the sands, the rest of what I feel is her story is verging on surmise, based on Arnold's hearsay. Perhaps fantasy is already taking over. Who will contradict me, at this point?)

Guiding children toward an appreciation of fine food and gracious dining is crucial to their social development, believes culinary historian Fisher, who recounts her own maiden foray into the world of fine cuisine in this excerpt from "The First Café."

The first time I ever went to a restaurant, the waiter, I have been told, thought me delightful and my little sister even more so, in spite of the sad truth that children to waiters are professionally hell.

She was four, and I was six. We behaved nicely; we spoke neither too high nor too low, we sat up straight, we spilled almost not at all, and at the end of the meal she said to our man, "Oh, I am so sorry to leave all these dishes for you to wash, and a nearly clean napkin too!" He, who already loved us, or so it appears in Apocrypha, grew dewy-eyed.

Whatever his feelings then, he took care of us for some thirty years more in one or another of the respectable restaurants in Southern California, and when I strolled, a little while ago, into a beach chop house, there he was, celebrating his last night in the profession, and we embraced and touched several glasses together before he left for his chicken farm. If he wanted to take time from his capons and his poults to write a book, I cannot help believing that he would speak kindly of the two little girls who got such a fine start under his snowy, flickering napkin.

That was in Los Angeles, at Marcel's, in 1914 or a little later. There were a few good small restaurants there at that time, a kind of backwater from San Francisco, undoubtedly. Marcel's was, according to my parents and a great many other hungry provincials, very good indeed. And *Pinafore* was playing a matinee at the Mason Opera House. So my mother took us twenty-five miles each way on the trolley to see it and have our first meal in public, which she and my father decided—with no dispute—should be as fine as possible. I can remember nothing about it until we were sitting in the small room lighted with candles behind pink silk lampshades, with incredible expanses of snow-white linen, and a forest of glasses sparkling everywhere at our eye level, and with a fine, thin-nosed man dressed in black to take care of us— only us.

I do not know if Mother ordered in advance. I do know that she threw any dietetic patterns overboard. It seemed almost unbearable that a little fire should burn there at our table so dangerously, under a silver pan, and that the man could lean over it with-

out going up in flames, and put the plates so tenderly before us with a napkin over his fingers, while candles flared in the middle of the day and people we
had never seen before ate in the same room, as if we
were invisible.

There was no mention of milk to drink, but instead we lifted the tall goblets of forbidden ice water
waveringly to our lips, and looked up over them at
the pink rose nodding in a silver vase between us and
the world. There may have been other things to eat,
but the chafing-dish chicken is all my sister and I can
remember now, and of course the wonderful waiter
who kept on remembering us too, after that first
hushed luncheon.

It was a good start for us, that is if, in a world of
shifting values, it is good to start two humans off
with such firm high ones. I often think of it, almost
as strongly as I did one day in Paris when I was
lunching in the back part of the Café de Paris and
saw that the table next to mine was being dressed
with particular care. Finally people came to sit at it: a
handsome, famous actor, his beautiful British wife

who was divorced from him and their two children.
The little girl was very English and of course lived
with her mother, and the little boy was completely
Parisian, as any reader of the gossip columns could
have told you. But they all spoke easily together and
were charming and happy. It was obviously a ren-
dezvous that had been kept often by the four
separated people, there in that opulent, gracious eating house.

The father and mother drank a cocktail and
talked pleasurably, while the children sipped with
courtesy at a very good sherry, enough to cover the
bottoms of their proper little glasses. I forget the rest
of the meal, but I sat long after I should have gone to
keep an appointment, watching the cautious delight
of the children at the rather elaborate dishes the waiters brought for them, and the quiet enjoyment of the
parents. I was watching myself and my little sister,
and feeling within me the way my mother and the
English mother must have felt before the wide eyes,
the hushed voices, and the trembling polite hands of
their children.

Anaïs Nin

(1903–1977)

Many writers keep journals, but Anaïs Nin's made her famous. She began keeping a diary at age eleven to amuse herself on a long shipboard journey from her childhood home of Barcelona to New York City, where she and her mother were starting a new life together. Nin's mother encouraged the journal-keeping habit to the extent that she had the notebooks bound in leather.

Nin's entire life was to prove the stuff of good story-telling, and she related it to her diaries with a wildly romantic intensity. By the age of twenty, she was also writing novels and plays. Her marriage to Hugh Guiler, a banker, took the pair to Paris. There she plunged into the artistic, bohemian milieu of the time, investigating the flourishing surrealist movement in art and literature. Her first book, *D.H. Lawrence: An Unprofessional Study* (1923), was written during this period, inspired by the passion-charged works of the British author of *Lady Chatterley's Lover* and other novels.

In Paris, Nin fell in love with the American writer Henry Miller. She supported him financially while he finished his novel *Tropic of Cancer* (1934) and helped him write the book's preface. She also had a liaison with his wife June. While pregnant with Miller's child, Nin went to see Otto Rank, a Freudian psychiatrist who specialized in disorders of the artist. (He tried—unsuccessfully—to break Nin's diary habit.) She became Rank's assistant in 1934 and actually saw patients, all the while continuing to send money to Henry Miller.

When Nin showed her avant-garde novels and stories to Miller, he declared, "It is either flawless, or else it is gibberish." Eager to share her work with the world, she established her own hand-set press to publish *Under a Glass Bell* (1944) and *Children of the Albatross* (1946). Eventually these works came to the attention of a young New York editor named Gore Vidal,

Anaïs Nin

who was instrumental in getting them published commercially. Nin bought up many copies to help increase sales.

It was Henry Miller who persuaded Nin to publish her journals. In a critical study, he wrote that this facet of her work "rearranges the world in terms of female honesty." In 1966, Harcourt, Brace & World published the first volume of *The Diary of Anaïs Nin*. She was sixty-three. Seven volumes followed between 1966 and 1980.

Nin's *Diary* brought her the French Prix Sevigne for autobiography in 1971. With her coquettish appeal, flamboyant clothing, and advocacy of free love, she became a popular speaker on college campuses in the early 1970s. Her florid writing style was even the subject of an affectionate parody book. By this time, she was living with a young man in Big Sur, California, where she died at the age of seventy-three.

After her death, two volumes of Nin's erotic stories—*Delta of Venus* and *Little Birds*, which she had written for a private client in the 1940s—became best-sellers. When they were published, critics hailed them as examples of "the new sensual writing by women"—something Nin had been doing all her life.

In this excerpt from the novel A Spy in the House of Love *(1954), the character Sabina finds a source of strength and personal identity in her clothes closet as she is shoring up her psychic resources to face the world.*

Before she awakened Sabina's dark eyes showed the hard light of precious stones through a slit in the eyelids, pure dark green beryl shining, not yet warmed by her feverishness.

Then instantly she was awake, on guard.

She did not awaken gradually, in abandon and trust to the new day. As soon as light or sound registered on her consciousness, danger was in the air and she sat up to meet its thrusts.

Her first expression was one of tension, which was not beauty. Just as anxiety dispersed the strength of the body, it also gave to the face a wavering, tremulous vagueness, which was not beauty, like that of a drawing out of focus.

Slowly what she composed with the new day was her own focus, to bring together body and mind. This was made with an effort, as if all the dissolutions and dispersions of her self the night before were difficult to reassemble. She was like an actress who must compose a face, an attitude to meet the day.

The eyebrow pencil was no mere charcoal emphasis on blond eyebrows, but a design necessary to balance a chaotic asymmetry. Make up and powder were not simply applied to heighten a porcelain texture, to efface the uneven swellings caused by sleep, but to smooth out the sharp furroughs designed by nightmares, to reform the contours and blurred surfaces of the cheeks, to erase the contradictions and conflicts which strained the clarity of the face's lines, disturbing the purity of its forms.

She must redesign the face, smooth the anxious brows, separate the crushed eyelashes, wash off the traces of secret interior tears, accentuate the mouth as upon a canvas, so it will hold its luxuriant smile.

Inner chaos, like those secret volcanoes which suddenly lift the neat furrows of a peacefully ploughed field, awaited behind all disorders of face, hair and costume, for a fissure through which to explode.

What she saw in the mirror now was a flushed, clear-eyed face, smiling, smooth, beautiful. The multiple acts of composure and artifice had merely dissolved her anxieties; now that she felt prepared to meet the day, her true beauty emerged which had been frayed and marred by anxiety.

She considered her clothes with the same weighing of possible external dangers as she had the new day which had entered through her closed windows and doors.

Believing in the danger which sprang from objects as well as people, which dress, which shoes, which coat demanded less of her panicked heart and body? For a costume was a challenge too, a discipline, a trap which once adopted could influence the actor.

She ended by choosing a dress with a hole in its sleeve. The last time she had worn it, she had stood before a restaurant which was too luxurious, too ostentatious, which she was frightened to enter, but instead of saying: "I am afraid to enter here," she had been able to say: "I can't enter here with a hole in my sleeve."

She selected her cape which seemed more protective, more enveloping.

Also the cape held within its folds something of what she imagined was a quality possessed exclusively by man: some dash, some audacity, some swagger of freedom denied to woman.

Nin creates a man's persona in this excerpt from the novel Collages *(1964).*

One night he walked on to the end of a natural rock jetty and came upon a shoal of seals. They swam, dived, clowned, but always crawled back to the rocks to have their young ones there. They kissed, barked, leaped, danced on their partly fused hind limbs. Their black eyes were like mirrors reflecting sea and sky, but the ogival shape of their eyelids gave them an air of compassion, almost as if they would weep with sympathy. Their tails were of little use except for swimming but they liked to shake their webbed flipper-like limbs as if they were about to fly.

Their fur shone like onyx, with dark blue shadows under the fins.

They greeted the man with cries of joy. By this time he was an old man. The sea had wrinkled his face so intricately, it was a surprise when his smile scattered the lines to shine through, like a beautiful glossy fish darting out of a fishing net.

The old man fed the seals, he settled near them in a cave, cooked his dinner, and rolled over and fell asleep with a new feeling of companionship.

One night several men came. They wanted to

catch the seals for a display in a pool in front of their restaurant. A publicity stunt which attracted the children. But the pool was small, it was surrounded by barbed wire and the old man did not want this to happen to his seals. So he warned them by an imitation of their cry and bark, and they dove quickly into the sea. By the time the men reached the end of the jetty the seals were gone. From then on the old man felt he was their guardian. No one could get through at night without walking through his bedroom. In spite of the tap-dancing of the waves, and the siren calls of the wind, the old man would hear the dangerous visitors and always had time to warn the seals in their own language.

The old man discovered the seal's names. They answered to Hilarious, Ebenezer, Ambrosius, Eulalee and Adolfo. But there was one seal whose name he did not know, who was too old when they first met. The old man did not have the courage to try out names on him, to see which one he answered to, for the seal could hardly move and it would have humiliated him.

One severe winter the old man's children began to worry about him, as he was growing old and rheumatic. One rainy day they came and forced him into their car, and took him to their home and fixed him up a bedroom.

The first night he slept on a bed, he fell off and broke his arm. As soon as his arm was well again he returned to the cave.

One night when he felt minor quakes were taking place in the area of his heart, he thought he was going to die, so he tried to crawl nearer to the seals, into the crevices where they slept. But they gently, compassionately, nosed him out of the place.

By then he resembled them so much, with his mustache, his rough oval eyebrows, his drooping eyelids, and his barking cough, that he thought they would help him to slide down the rocks and be buried at sea, like a true seal.

Simone de Beauvoir

(1908–1986)

"One is not born a woman, one becomes one," wrote France's most distinguished female author in *The Second Sex* (1949), her groundbreaking study of the place of women in society. Beauvoir's landmark book would later inspire such important feminist thinkers of the 1970s as Kate Millett and Germaine Greer with its unflinching scrutiny of the myriad myths that have surrounded womanhood throughout history.

As a child, Simone de Beauvoir had been encouraged to pursue a career. The elder of two daughters, she grew up in a middle-class Catholic family in Paris. After a formal education she went on to study philosophy at the Sorbonne, where she met the philosopher Jean-Paul Sartre, who was to become her longtime companion. Beauvoir spent nearly fifteen years as a secondary-school instructor in Marseilles, Rouen, and Paris. During this period, she wrote several novels, including *L'Invite (She Came to Stay)*, published in 1943. She bore no children, and her relationship with Sartre's adopted daughter is said to have been stormy.

Beauvoir's association with Sartre thrust her into an exciting world of ideas. Together the pair began the philosophical movement known as Existentialism. It stressed the individual's position as a self-determining being responsible for one's own choices and able to set the limits of his or her freedom.

Once she dedicated herself to writing full-time, Beauvoir published numerous essays and novels, plus a five-volume autobiography. *The Mandarins* (1957), a dramatic tale set against a backdrop of French left-wing politics in the postwar years, won her the coveted Prix Goncourt, the highest French literary honor. The book is based on Beauvoir's own life and borrows heavily from the story of her involvement with a certain American writer (who in real life was the novelist Nelson Algren) and how she refused to marry him because of her responsibility to her husband. Philosophers Albert Camus and Arthur Koestler also appear in the book in thinly disguised cameos.

The Second Sex, published in the United States in 1953, remains Beauvoir's most famous book. Clearly influenced by the hard thinking of Existentialism, this study attempts to demonstrate how women internalize negative assumptions about themselves—including the assumption that they are biologically inferior to men. Although the book addresses some painfully honest truths about the inherent difficulties of maintaining male-female relationships, The Second Sex is, ironically, regarded by some scholars today as being somewhat sexist. In writing it, Beauvoir simply took for granted certain notions about the natural differences between the sexes, unquestioned during the 1950s, that are no longer accepted.

Beauvoir always had a fierce interest in politics. After World War II she adopted a left-wing and sometime dangerous stance on French policy in Algeria and later spoke out against U.S. involvement in Vietnam. But until the 1970s, her involvement with feminism was largely intellectual. Once the fervor of the women's movement hit France she became one of its most vocal supporters, calling for a woman's rights to abortion and protection against domestic violence. After Sartre died in 1980, she remained involved in many friendships and causes and was honored extensively in her lifetime.

Beauvoir, whose Second Sex *caused the first rumblings of the modern feminist movement, also wrote fiction. In* The Woman Destroyed *(1969), set in a beautifully described French countryside, she relates the unrest of a woman who, now that her children have grown up and moved away, has been looking forward to new joys with her husband. But once away, she makes a disturbing discovery.*

Monday 1 November.

It was so like the past: I almost believed the likeness was going to bring the past to life again. We had driven through fog and then beneath a beautiful cold sun. At Bar-le-Duc and at Saint-Mihiel we looked at Ligier Richier's sculptures again, and we were as deeply moved as we had been in the old days: it was I who showed them to him first. Since then we have traveled quite a lot; we have seen a great deal; and yet the "Décharné" astonished us all over again. In Nancy, as we stood in front of the wrought-iron rail-ings of the Place Stanislas, I felt something piercing in my heart—a happiness that hurt, so unaccustomed had it become. In those old country-town streets I squeezed his arm under mine; or sometimes he put his around my shoulders.

We talked about everything, and about nothing, and about our daughters a great deal. He cannot bring himself to understand how Colette could have married Jean-Pierre: with her chemistry and biology he had planned a brilliant career for her; and we should have given her complete romantic and sexual

Simone de Beauvoir

freedom, as she knew. Why had she fallen for such a totally commonplace young fellow—fallen for him to the point of giving up her whole future to him?

"She is happy that way," I said.

"I should have preferred her to be happy some other way."

The going of Lucienne, his favorite, saddens him still more. Although he approves of her liking for independence, he would have preferred her to stay in Paris; he would have preferred her to read medicine and work with him.

"Then she would not have been independent."

"Oh, yes, she would. She would have had her own life at the same time as she worked with me."

Fathers never have exactly the daughters they want because they invent a notion of them that the daughters have to conform to. Mothers accept them as they are. Colette needed security above all, and Lucienne needed freedom: I understand them both. And I think each perfectly successful in her own way—Colette so sensitive and kind, Lucienne so brilliant, so full of energy.

We stopped at the same little hotel we had stayed at twenty years ago, and we had—perhaps on another floor—the same room. I went to bed first, and I watched him, walking to and fro in his blue pajamas, barefooted on the worn carpet. He looked neither cheerful nor sad. And I was blinded by the mental image—an image called up hundreds of times, set, but not worn out, still shining with newness—of Maurice walking barefoot upon this carpet in his black pajamas: he had pulled up the collar and its points framed his face; he talked nonsense, childishly

worked up. I realized that I had come here in the hope of once more finding that man so hopelessly in love: I had not seen him for years and years, although this memory lies like a transparency over all the visions I have of him. That evening, for the very reason that the surroundings were the same, the old image, coming into contact with a flesh and blood man smoking a cigarette, fell to dust and ashes. I had a shattering revelation: *time goes by*. I began to weep. He sat on the edge of the bed and took me tenderly in his arms. "Sweetheart, my sweetheart, don't cry. What are you crying for?" He stroked my hair; he gave me little fluttering kisses on the side of my head.

"It's nothing; it's over," I said. "I'm fine."

I was fine; the room was bathed in a pleasant twilight, Maurice's hands and mouth were soft; I put my lips to his; and I slipped my hand under his pajama jacket. And suddenly he was upright. he had thrust me away with a sudden jerk. I whispered, "Do I disgust you as much as all that?"

"You're out of your mind, darling! But I'm dropping with tiredness. It's the open air—walking about. I just have to sleep."

I buried myself under the blankets. He lay down. He turned out the light. I had the feeling of being at the bottom of a grave, with the blood frozen in my veins, unable either to stir or to weep. We had not made love since Mougins: and even then, that could hardly be called making love. . . . About four o'clock I dropped off. When I woke up he was coming back into the bedroom, fully dressed: it was nine or thereabouts. I asked him where he had been.

"I went for a stroll."

But it was raining outside, and he did not have his raincoat with him; he was not wet. He had been to telephone Noëllie. She had insisted upon his telephoning: she didn't even have the generosity to let me have him all to myself even for one wretched weekend. I said nothing. The day dragged along. Each realized that the other was making an effort to be pleasant and cheerful. We both agreed to go back to Paris for dinner and finish the evening at the cinema.

Why had he thrust me from him? Men still try to pick me up in the street; they squeeze my knee in the cinema. I have fattened a little—not much. My bosom went to pieces after Lucienne's birth; but ten years ago it stirred Maurice. And two years ago Quillan was wild to go to bed with me. No. The reason why Maurice jerked away was that he is infatuated with Noëllie; he could not bear sleeping with another woman. If he has her under his skin to that degree, and if at the same time he lets himself be dazzled by her, things are far more serious than I had imagined.

Eudora Welty

Eudora Welty

(born 1909)

Steely of will, belying those magnolia-sweet stereotypes, Southern women take a central role in many short stories by Eudora Welty. From nine-year-old Lauren McRaven, the precocious observer of *Delta Wedding*, listening wide-eyed as her elders graphically recount the facts of childbirth, to New York career woman Laurel Hand of *The Optimist's Daughter*, whose return to Mississippi for her father's funeral occasions a wrenching look at her past, Welty's female characters ring true to their Southern roots.

These women know the minutiae of housework as intimately as they know the lines on their hard-used hands. Unvarnished truths about pregnancy, motherhood, and the homemaker's lot tumble off their lips. The American South has a long, rich heritage of storytelling, and the women in *The Bride of the Innisfallen, and Other Stories* (1954), and other Welty books, recount their wisdom with spare eloquence. They are also conversant with the mystical world, as befits denizens of the delta region near Welty's birthplace of Jackson, Mississippi, where centuries-old forms of voodoo are kept alive by some practitioners.

Welty attended Mississippi State College for Women, graduated in 1929 from the University of Wisconsin, and earned a master's degree in business administration from Columbia University two years later. After that it was back home to Mississippi and a job as a small-town journalist. In this capacity, Welty reported on Jackson's social events for a local newspaper and edited news broadcasts for a radio show.

The Works Progress Administration, a federal agency formed to institute and administrate public works as a way of relieving the unemployment woes of the Great Depression, had just been established. Welty found work as a WPA photographer and reporter, creating what amounted to an oral history of the American South as she snapped residents' pictures and recorded the stories they told of their families' lives.

These journalistic examinations of Southern folk tales and traditions echoed in the short stories Welty began to write in 1936. Another strong influence was the novelist Katherine Ann Porter, the author of *Ship of Fools*, who had become Welty's literary mentor. In fact, it was Porter who encouraged her to explore fiction. And explore she did, in numerous volumes beginning with *The Wide Net, and Other Stories* (1943). One of Welty's most celebrated is *Delta Wedding* (1946), which affectionately captures the details of women's domestic pursuits as they prepare for the marriage of Troy Flavin and Dabney Fairchild.

Welty received the Pulitzer Prize for literature for *The Optimist's Daughter*, a deceptively straightforward tale about the tangled love between a mother and her daughter published in 1972. Welty's protagonist, a self-sufficient working woman who returns to Mississippi for her father's funeral, comes to identify with her dead mother's quest for independence. Reconciliation with the painful memory of her mother makes Laurel Hand much stronger for the experience. Like many of Welty's women characters, Laurel, in the end, is fully capable of taking care of herself.

You can take the woman out of the South, but you cannot take the South out of the woman—at least not in The Optimist's Daughter, *Welty's moving story of Laurel McKelva Hand, who returns to her native New Orleans from the North when her father falls ill. In this excerpt, she revisits the home of her youth and confronts her troubled past.*

Firelight and warmth—that was what her memory gave her. Where the secretary was now there had been her small bed, with its railed sides that could be raised as tall as she was when she stood up in bed, arms up to be lifted out. The sewing machine was still in place under the single window. When her mother—or, at her rare, appointed times, the sewing woman—sat here in her chair pedalling and whirring, Laurel sat on this floor and put together the fallen scraps of cloth into stars, flowers, birds, people, or whatever she liked to call them, lining them up, spacing them out, making them into patterns, families, on the sweet-smelling matting, with the shine of firelight, or the summer light, moving over mother and child and what they both were making.

It was quieter here. It was around the corner from the wind, and a room away from the bird and the disturbed dark. It seemed as far from the rest of the house itself as Mount Salus was from Chicago.

Laurel sat down on the slipper chair. The goose-neck lamp threw its dimmed beam on the secretary's warm brown doors. It had been made of the cherry trees on the McKelva place a long time ago; on the lid, the numerals 1817 had been set into a not quite perfect oval of different wood, something smooth and yellow as a scrap of satin. It had been built as a plantation desk but was graceful and small enough for a lady's use; Laurel's mother had had entire claim on it. On its pediment stood a lead-mold eagle spreading its wings and clasping the globe: it was about the same breadth as her mother's spread-out hand. There was no key in either keyhole of the double doors of the cabinet. But had there ever been a key? Her mother had never locked up anything that Laurel could remember. Her privacy was keyless. She had simply assumed her privacy. Now, suppose that again she would find everything was gone?

Laurel had hesitated coming to open her father's desk; she was not hesitating here—not now. She touched the doors where they met, and they swung open together. Within, the cabinet looked like a little wall out of a country post office which nobody had in years disturbed by calling for their mail. How had her mother's papers lain under merciful dust in the years past and escaped destruction? Laurel was sure of why: her father could not have borne to touch them; to Fay, they would have been only what somebody wrote—and anybody reduced to the need to write, Fay would think already beaten as a rival.

Laurel opened out the writing lid, and reaching up she drew down the letters and papers from one pigeonhole at a time. There were twenty-six pigeonholes, but her mother had stored things according to their time and place, she discovered, not by ABC. Only the letters from her father had been all brought together, all she had received in her life, surely—there

they were; the oldest envelopes had turned saffron. Laurel drew a single one out, opened the page inside long enough to see it beginning "My darling Sweetheart," and returned it to its place. They were postmarked from the courthouse towns her father had made sojourn in, and from Mount Salus when he addressed them to West Virginia on her visits "up home"; and under these were the letters to Miss Becky Thurston, tied in ribbons that were almost transparent, and freckled now, as the skin of her mother's hands came to be before she died. In the back of the pigeonhole where these letters came from was some solid little object, and Laurel drew it out, her fingers remembering it before she held it under her eyes. It was a two-inch bit of slatey stone, given shape by many little strokes from a penknife. It had come out of its cranny the temperature and smoothness of her skin; it fitted into her palm. "A little dish!" Laurel the child had exclaimed, thinking it something made by a child younger than she. "A boat," corrected her mother importantly. The initials C.C.M.McK. were cut running together into the base. Her father had made it himself. It had gone from his hand to her mother's; that was a river stone; they had been courting, "up home."

There was a careful record of those days preserved in a snapshot book. Laurel felt along the shelf above the pigeonholes and touched it, the square boards, the silk tassel. She pulled it down to her.

Still clinging to the first facing pages were the pair of grayed and stippled home-printed snapshots: Clinton and Becky "up home," each taken by the other standing in the same spot on a railroad track (a leafy glade), he slender as a wand, his foot on a milepost, swinging his straw hat; she with her hands full of the wildflowers they'd picked along the way.

"The most beautiful blouse I ever owned in my life—I made it. Cloth from Mother's own spinning, and dyed a deep, rich, American Beauty color with pokeberries," her mother had said with the gravity in which she spoke of "up home." "I'll never have anything to wear that to me is as satisfactory as that blouse."

How darling and vain she was when she was young! Laurel thought now. She'd made the blouse— and developed the pictures too, for why couldn't she? And very likely she had made the paste that held them.

Doris Lessing

(born 1919)

Few female authors have taken on as much of the world in their work as the British novelist Doris Lessing. Her numerous works of fiction are set in disparate areas of a flawed, violent earth—and even beyond it in her later, visionary pieces set in the future. One of modern literature's most intelligent voices, she has written passionately about aging, child-rearing, madness, politics, space travel, men and women, and the other confusions of the world in which we live.

Born Doris May Tayler in Persia, Lessing moved with her British parents to southern Rhodesia (now Zimbabwe) at the age of five. She left school at fifteen to work as a governess, typist, and telephone operator. Observing the racial strife in British colonial Africa instilled in Lessing a strong political consciousness. She became involved in radical politics after the breakup of her first marriage, joining the Communist party in 1944. She remained a member until 1956, after she had moved with her youngest child to England, where she lives today.

African Stories (1948) and *Going Home* (1949), Lessing's earliest works, were semi-autobiographical stories set in the Africa she both loved and despised. *The Grass Is Singing* (1950), which takes place in Rhodesia, was the first novel in her five-volume Children of Violence series. Spanning five decades and two continents, it recounts the life of a character named Martha Quest, beginning in her African adolescence and ending in an apocalyptic future.

Lessing's masterpiece is *The Golden Notebook* (1962), a pioneering work of the feminist movement. In it, she explores such seemingly disparate subjects as writer's block and female politics through the vision of Anna Wulf, a writer who compartmentalizes her life into four different notebooks. Anna struggles to make her way independently in a world that sometimes threatens to diminish her. Kate Brown, the protagonist of *The Summer Before the Dark* (1973), is a proper South London wife and mother who spends a season on her own for the first time since she married as a teenager. Kate finds herself amidst a maelstrom of activity ranging from global politics to power shortages to late 1960s hippie culture: "You see, it's not often that I get the chance to be absolutely free, and not to have to do things, look after things. I don't know when I shall have it again!"

Politics is just one of many influences on Lessing's prolific output of fiction. Psychiatry is another. In the mid-1960s she was a patient of the radical therapist R.D. Laing, drawing on the experience in *Briefing for a Descent into Hell* (1971). She also examined male-female relationships in the collection of novellas *A Man and Two Women* (1965) and the novel *The Story of a Non-Marrying Man* (1972).

In recent years, Lessing has offered expansive appraisals of global conditions. Her interest in Sufi mysticism led to a five-volume series of visionary "space-fiction" books called *Canopus in Argos: Archives*, written between 1979 and 1983. She has also taken a political activist's stance in such works as *The Good Terrorist* (1985) and continues to speak and write about issues of importance to her.

In The Summer Before the Dark, *the well-to-do, middle-aged British housewife Kate Brown ventures out into the world on her own for the first time since she married and had children. In this excerpt, Kate alternately experiences bewilderment and empowerment as she begins her new job as an interpreter for a large international economic conference.*

In this room were decided the fates and fortunes of millions of little people, what crops they were going to grow, what they would eat and wear—and think.

While Charlie Cooper was still laying a sheet of paper—the apology, miraculously multiplied in this brief space of a few minutes—in each place around the table, the delegates came in, laughing and talking. What an extraordinarily attractive lot they were! Such a collection of many-coloured, many-nationed handsome men and women would be what a film producer would try to shoot to make a scene from some idealised picture of united nations. But would the actors have been able to convey such a perfection of casual authority, such assurance? For that was the impression they made. The difference between them and their assistants and secretaries and the attendants of various kinds could be seen by that quality alone. Each man or woman strolled to his or her chair, seated himself, continued to talk and to laugh with a perfection of ease that shouted the one word: *Power.* Every gesture, each look, conveyed conviction of usefulness, the weight of what they represented.

Some of the clothes worn were national costume: there were half a dozen men and women from somewhere in Africa who made all the others look members of inferior races, so tall and graceful and majestically dressed were they: the folds of their

Doris Lessing

robes, their earrings, the turn of a head—each knew its role. And what authority even the creases in a suit can convey, worn by a man whose decisions are of importance to people hauling sacks of coffee on a hillside thousands of miles away.

The proceedings had begun; and Kate found that her brain, that machine, was doing its work smoothly. A few moments of panic, a feeling that her mind was blank and would be forever, had been dispelled by hearing her own words come out, quite sensibly ordered, and by watching the faces of the people who listened. No one seemed upset by what they heard; everything was as it should be.

And in an incredibly short time—it turned out that it had been two hours—she was relieved by a colleague, was sent off to relax and have a good lunch. She returned to her cubicle with confidence; and by five o'clock that afternoon felt as much a part of this organisation as she did of her family. To which she returned too late for the evening meal, to find that her daughter had cooked it and that everything was going on quite comfortably.

By the end of that week Kate was initiated into the complexities of that bitter and fragrant herb the world drinks so much of; she could hardly think of anything else. And her house had been tidied and put ready for letting. Then it had been let, until the end of September, and the family had departed to its various destinations without any help from her. All she had said was, in a voice which only a week before would have been anxious, but now was indifferent, "Someone has got to see to it, because I haven't got the time." She had kissed her husband, and her three sons and her daughter goodbye, but had not yet time to feel any particular emotion.

She was in a room in a flat rented by one of her colleagues; a woman who had translated, but who had been promoted: she now organised conferences. This move from Kate's home into this room, with all the necessities for some months, had taken half an hour, and the act of flinging some clothes into a suitcase.

None of the clothes were any use, anyway. At some point during that week she rushed out to buy the dresses that would admit her, like a passport, to this way of life. Mrs. Michael Brown could not have been called ill-dressed; but it was not Mrs. Michael Brown who was being employed by Global Food.

Before going shopping she had asked Charlie Cooper what she was going to earn. His round, humorous, harassed face—his permanent expression, because of being male nanny to so many committees—became agonised with remorse.

"My dear!" he said. "Accept my apologies! Oh, I don't see how you can—it was really too awful of me! I should have talked about that before anything else. But it's been such a week—really, if you only knew what a godsend you've been!" And he mentioned a sum which she stopped herself exclaiming at. It was in this casual, positively gentlemanly way, as if the world of trade unions, of bitterly contested wages, poverty, the anguish of hunger, did not exist, that the salaries of these international officials, these indispensable fortunates, could be arranged.

She had bought her dresses, half a dozen of them, thinking that at the end of her two weeks with Global Food, she would have a wardrobe fit for an elegant holiday somewhere. But her plans were only for, perhaps, visiting an old friend in Sussex, or an aunt in Scotland. She had not really thought of what she was going to do.

The second week was less pressured. Her work had become something she did as easily as she had run a home—unbelievably, only a few days ago. She did it automatically. In between the sessions in the cubicles, she spent her time in the coffee rooms, watching. She was, after all, an outsider, did not feel that she was entitled to join this privileged throng. She was a migrant; it would be all over in a week. But she sat as if she felt she had a right to it all—her new dresses made this much easier; she drank the superb coffee, she watched. It was like a market. Or like a long, gay, permanently continuing party.

A woman sat in the public room, relaxed but observant, an official in a public organisation, dressed like one, holding herself like one; but letting her life—or the words that represented her thoughts about her life—flow through her mind. Was it that for twenty-five years she had been part of that knot of tension, the family, and had forgotten that ordinary life, life for everyone not in the family, was so agreeable, so undemanding? How well-dressed everyone was. How everybody's skin glowed and shone. And how easy the way a man or a woman would come in here, glance around, find smiles and pleasant looks waiting for them, then wave and sit down by themselves, with a gesture that said: *I need a moment's solitude*—which wish was of course respected. Or casually, almost insolently, look over the room to see which group he or she would join. There seemed never a sign of the tension that you would find after five minutes in any street outside this sheltered place. In any street, or shop, or home the currents flowed and crossed and made new currents. Outside this great public building the conflicts went on. But here? Had these easy well-turned creatures, each burnished and polished by money, ever suffered? Ever wept in the dark? Ever wanted something they could not get? Off course they had, they must have—but there was not a sign of it. Had they ever—but perhaps this was not the right question to ask—had they ever been hungry?

Nadine Gordimer

Nadine Gordimer

(born 1923)

*I*n South Africa, the difficult politics of race are impossible to ignore. Most of the works of novelist and short story writer Nadine Gordimer are informed by her outspoken opposition to the apartheid and censorship she has witnessed first-hand since childhood.

Gordimer was born in Springs, a mining town outside Johannesburg, to Jewish parents who had emigrated from London. Her mother, she has written, was a neurotic invalid who demanded Nadine's presence at her side whenever possible. To escape this repression, the young Nadine began to write stories and lose herself in library books. By age fifteen she had a story published in a local magazine. After graduating from the local private schools and university, she dedicated herself to literature. In her early twenties, *Harper's* came calling, and *The New Yorker* bought a story when she was twenty-eight, beginning a decades-long association and ensuring Gordimer an avid audience of American readers.

Gordimer married for the first time in 1949, the same year her short-story volume, *Face to Face*, was published. Its tales are populated with both black and white South Africans who endure the consequences and distortions of racial oppression. This theme continues in her first novel, *The Lying Days* (1953), about a young white woman raised in Johannesburg suburb. Commenting on *The Lying Days*, a *New York Times* reviewer enthusiastically compared Gordimer to Virginia Woolf. Following the dissolution of her first marriage in 1954, Gordimer wed an art gallery owner, with whom she later collaborated on one of her numerous television plays and documentaries. She has a son and a daughter.

Gordimer's voluminous body of work includes *A World of Strangers* (1958), the well-received story collection *Friday's Footprint, and Other Stories* (1960), and *The Late Bourgeois World*

(1966). *A Guest of Honor* (1970) concerns a British colonial officer who returns to the country from which he had been expelled for supporting the black South African community.

Gordimer has always taken very seriously her responsibility as a South African writer. *Burger's Daughter* (1979), a moving tale about the personal and political heritage of Rose Burger, whose communist father had died in prison, was the third of her books to be banned there. In response, Gordimer published a pamphlet entitled *What Happened to Burger's Daughter: or, How South African Censorship Works*. When the repression of literature abated somewhat, she helped organize the Anti-Censorship Action Group, dedicated to exposing censorship within the daily press and the electronic media.

Critics hailed Gordimer's ironic short novel *July's People* (1981), a work set in an unsettling near future. It follows a white family who, in fleeing civil war, become dependent for safety upon their black servants. To date, she had published nearly two dozen books, while traveling occasionally to the U.S. as a visiting university professor.

In 1991, she won the Nobel Prize for literature. Today, Gordimer continues to live outside Johannesburg, in the country whose physical beauty and character she has always loved and whose politics she has impacted with her superbly written words.

Her native South Africa may be a country divided by politics, but the characters in Gordimer's novella Something Out There *(1979) transcend their differences by cutting to the core of human emotion. Here, a white Johannesburg couple awaits the arrival of two black revolutionaries, whose cause they support as their own.*

The white couple had known two black men would be coming but not exactly when or how. Charles must have believed they would come at night, that would be the likeliest because the safest; the first three nights in the house he dragged the mattress off her bed into the kitchen, and his into the "lounge", on which the front door opened directly, so that he or she would hear the men wherever they sought entry. Charles had great difficulty in sleeping with one eye open; he could stay awake until very late, but once his head was on a pillow sleep buried him deep within the hot, curly beard. She dozed off where she was—meetings, cinemas, parties, even driving—after around half-past ten, but she could give her subconscious instructions, before going to bed, to wake her at any awaited signal of sound or movement. She set her inner alarm at hair-trigger, those three nights. An owl sent her swiftly to Charles; it might be a man imitating the call. She responded to a belch from the sink drain, skittering in the roof (mice?), even the faint thread of a cat's mew, that might have been in a dream, since she could not catch it again once it had awakened her.

But they came at two o'clock on the fourth afternoon. A small sagging van of the kind used by the petty entrepreneurs in firewood and junk commerce, *dagga*-running, livestock and human transport between black communities on either side of the borders with Swaziland, Lesotho or Botswana, backed down to the gate it had overshot. There were women and children with blankets covering their mouths against the dust in the open rear. A young man jumped from the cab and dragged aside the sagging, silvery wire-and-scroll gate, with its plate "Plot 185 Koppiesdrif". Charles was out the front door and reversing the initiative at once: he it was who came to the man. His green eyes, at twenty-eight, already were narrowed by the plump fold of the lower lid that marks joviality—whether cruelly shrewd or good-natured—in middle age. The young black man was chewing gum. He did not interrupt the rhythms of his jaw:—Charles.—

The couple had not been told what the men would look like. The man identified himself by the procedure (questions and specific answers) Charles had been taught to expect. Charles asked whether they wouldn't drive round to the yard. The other understood at once; it was more natural for blacks to conduct any business with a white man at his back door. Charles himself was staging the arrival in keeping with the unremarkable deliveries of building material that already had been made to the new occupiers of the plot. He walked ahead of the van, business-like. In the yard another young man got out of the cab, and, with the first, from among the women swung down two zippered carry-alls and a crammed paper carrier. That was all.

The women and children, like sheep dazed by their last journey to the abattoir, moved only when the van drove off again, jolting them.

Charles and the girl had not been told the names or identity of the pair they expected. They exchanged only first names—Eddie was the one who had opened the gate, Vusi the one who had sat beside the unknown driver and got down in the yard. The girl introduced herself as "Joy". One of the men asked if there was something to eat. The white couple at once got in one another's way, suddenly unrehearsed now that the reality had begun, exchanging terse instructions in the kitchen, jostling one another to find sugar, a knife to slice tomatoes, a frying pan for the sausages which she forgot to prick. It seemed there was no special attitude, social formula of ease, created by a situation so far removed from the normal pattern of human concourse; so it was just the old, inappropriate one of stilted hospitality to unexpected guests that had to do, although these were not guests, the white couple were not hosts, and the arrival was according to plan. When sleeping arrangements came up, the men assumed the white couple were sleeping together and put their own things in the second bedroom. It was small and dark, unfurnished except for two new mattresses on the floor separated by an old trunk with a reading lamp standing on it, but there was no question of the other two favouring themselves with a better room; this one faced on the yard, no one would see blacks moving around at night in the bedroom of a white man's house.

The two zippered carry-alls, cheap copies of the hand luggage of jet-flight holiday-makers, held a change of jeans, a couple of shirts printed with bright leisure symbols of the Caribbean, a few books, and—in Eddie's—a mock-suède jacket with Indian fringes, Wild West style. As soon as they all knew each other well enough, he was teased about it, and had his quick riposte.—But I'm not going to be extinct.—The strong paper carrier was one of those imprinted with a pop star's face black kids shake for sale on the street corners of Johannesburg. What came out of it, the white couple saw, was as ordinary as the loaves of bread and cardboard litres of *mageu* such bags usually carry; a transistor-tape player, Vusi's spare pair of sneakers, a pink towel and a plastic briefcase emptied of papers. Charles was to provide everything they might need. He himself had been provided with a combi. He went to the appointed places, at appointed times, to pick up what was necessary.

The combi had housewifely curtains across the windows—a practical adornment popular with farming families, whose children may sleep away a journey. It was impossible to tell, when Charles drove off or came back, whether there was anything inside it. On one of his return trips, he drew up at the level crossing and found himself beside Naas Klopper and Mrs. Naas in the Mercedes. A train shuttered past like a camera gone berserk, lens opening and closing, with each flying segment of rolling stock, on flashes of the veld behind it. The optical explosion invigorated Charles. He waved and grinned at the estate agent and his wife.

Flannery O'Connor

(1925–1964)

A rainbow-feathered peacock has come to symbolize the Georgia-born novelist and short-story writer Flannery O'Connor. She raised peafowl on her family's farm and spent, at her own admission, a great deal of time observing their behavior as they strutted around the barnyard.

An only child, O'Connor grew up among itinerant farm workers and country folks who knew how to spin out a story. After graduation from a women's college in her hometown of Milledgeville, O'Connor went north at age twenty-two, to the University of Iowa's School for Writers. In 1948, she became a writer-in-residence at Yaddo, the foundation estate in Saratoga Springs, New York, which supported promising artists. There she worked on the stories which appeared in her first collection, *A Good Man Is Hard to Find* (1955). The second, *Everything That Rises Must Converge*, was published ten years later. O'Connor was already at work on longer pieces, but acknowledged to a friend that she was a very slow writer. "I don't have my novel outlined and I have to write to discover what I am doing," she explained.

O'Connor's work is often described as Southern Gothic, in the same stylistic vein as William Faulkner and Carson McCullers. These writers took their inspiration from the regional mysteries and peculiarities of the deep South—its characters, language, and ways of life. Before a public reading of her work, O'Connor once said, "I doubt if the texture of Southern life is any more grotesque than that of the rest of the nation, but it does seem evident that the Southern writer is particularly adept at recognizing the grotesque."

She also remarked that her Catholicism—unusual in an area populated largely by Baptists and Protestants—informed her work with a particular freedom to follow a vision and tell a story. In her first novel, *Wise Blood* (1962), O'Connor wrote freely about a violent young

Flannery O'Connor

religious extremist. *The Violent Bear It Away* (1960) also deals with fanaticism. So do several of her earlier pieces, collected in *The Complete Stories*. Published in 1971, this anthology won a posthumous National Book Award. Also released after her death was *Mystery and Manners: Occasional Prose.*

After Yaddo, O'Connor lived briefly with friends who invited her to their large country estate in Connecticut, a conducive place in which to write. She returned to Georgia after being diagnosed with disseminated lupus erythematosus, an incurable metabolic disease. Costly steroid drugs helped keep the symptoms under control, though her movements were greatly restricted. She lived the rest of her life on her mother's farm, where the two women raised chickens and peacocks while O'Connor worked at her novels. As in her stories, she observed the situation with fatalistic wit. "I am going to be the World Authority on Peafowl," she once wrote to Robert Lowell and his wife, "and I hope to be offered a chair some day at the Chicken College."

It's high time she gave up her racist old ways, Julian tells his mother angrily, as she condescends to a black child in the short story "Everything That Rises Must Converge." O'Connor's setting is her native South, at the beginning of the civil rights movement. All too soon, Julian is made to see the painful, horrible consequences of his anger.

"Oh little boy!" Julian's mother called and took a few quick steps and caught up with them just beyond the lamppost. "Here's a bright new penny for you," and she held out the coin, which shone bronze in the dim light.

The huge woman turned and for a moment stood, her shoulders lifted and her face frozen with frustrated rage, and stared at Julian's mother. Then all at once she seemed to explode like a piece of machinery that had been given one ounce of pressure too much. Julian saw the black fist swing out with the red pocketbook. He shut his eyes and cringed as he heard the woman shout, "He don't take nobody's pennies!" When he opened his eyes, the woman was disappearing down the street with the little boy staring wide-eyed over her shoulder. Julian's mother was sitting on the sidewalk.

"I told you not to do that," Julian said angrily. "I told you not to do that!"

He stood over her for a minute, gritting his teeth. Her legs were stretched out in front of her and her hat was on her lap. He squatted down and looked her in the face. It was totally expressionless. "You got exactly what you deserved," he said. "Now get up."

He picked up her pocketbook and put what had fallen out back in it. He picked the hat up off her lap. The penny caught his eye on the sidewalk and he picked that up and let it drop before her eyes into the purse. Then he stood up and leaned over and held his hands out to pull her up. She remained immobile. He sighed. Rising above them on either side were black apartment buildings, marked with irregular rectangles of light. At the end of the block a man came out of a door and walked off in the opposite direction.

"All right," he said, "suppose somebody happens by and wants to know why you're sitting on the sidewalk?"

She took the hand and, breathing hard, pulled heavily up on it and then stood for a moment, swaying slightly as if the spots of light in the darkness were circling around her. Her eyes, shadowed and confused, finally settled on his face. He did not try to conceal his irritation. "I hope this teaches you a lesson," he said. She leaned forward and her eyes raked his face. She seemed trying to determine his identity. Then, as if she found nothing familiar about him, she started off with a headlong movement in the wrong direction.

"Aren't you going on to the Y?" he asked.

"Home," she muttered.

"Well, are we walking?"

For answer she kept going. Julian followed along, his hands behind him. He saw no reason to let the lesson she had had go without backing it up with an explanation of its meaning. She might as well be made to understand what had happened to her. "Don't think that was just an uppity Negro woman," he said. "That was the whole colored race which will no longer take your condescending pennies. That was your black double. She can wear the same hat as you, and to be sure," he added gratuitously (because he thought it was funny), "it looked better on her than it did on you. What all this means," he said, "is that the old world is gone. The old manners are obsolete and your graciousness is not worth a damn." He thought bitterly of the house that had been lost for him. "You aren't who you think you are," he said.

She continued to plow ahead, paying no attention to him. Her hair had come undone on one side. She dropped her pocketbook and took no notice. He stooped and picked it up and handed it to her but she did not take it.

"You needn't act as if the world had come to an end," he said, "because it hasn't. From now on you've got to live in a new world and face a few realities for a change. Buck up," he said, "it won't kill you."

She was breathing fast.

"Let's wait on the bus," he said.

"Home," she said thickly.

"I hate to see you behave like this," he said. "Just like a child. I should be able to expect more of you." He decided to stop where he was and make her stop and wait for a bus. "I'm not going any farther," he said, stopping. "We're going on the bus."

She continued to go on as if she had not heard him. He took a few steps and caught her arm and stopped her. He looked into her face and caught his breath. He was looking into a face he had never seen before. "Tell Grandpa to come get me," she said.

He stared, stricken.

"Tell Caroline to come get me," she said.

Stunned, he let her go and she lurched forward again, walking as if one leg were shorter than the other. A tide of darkness seemed to be sweeping her from him. "Mother!" he cried. "Darling, sweetheart, wait!" Crumpling, she fell to the pavement. He dashed forward and fell at her side, crying, "Mamma, Mamma!" He turned her over. Her face was fiercely distorted. One eye, large and staring, moved slightly to the left as if it had become unmoored. The other remained fixed on him, raked his face again, found nothing and closed.

"Wait here, wait here!" he cried and jumped up and began to run for help toward a cluster of lights he saw in the distance ahead of him. "Help, help!" he shouted, but his voice was thin, scarcely a thread of sound. The lights drifted farther away the faster he ran and his feet moved numbly as if they carried him nowhere. The tide of darkness seemed to sweep him back to her, postponing from moment to moment his entry into the world of guilt and sorrow.

Ursula K. Le Guin

Ursula K. Le Guin

(born 1929)

"**F**irst sentences are doors to worlds," observed Ursula K. Le Guin, a science fiction writer and the only author to have won three Nebulas and four Hugos (the major science fiction prizes) as well as the National Book Award. Le Guin has proven the power of the first sentence in an awesome assortment of novels, stories, verses, essays, and scripts for film and radio.

Born in Berkeley, California, Le Guin grew up with three siblings. Her parents, who were anthropologists, were also inclined toward the literary life. Le Guin's mother, at the age of fifty-five, began writing children's stories and nonfiction accounts of Native American life, and her father was an occasional collaborator. Le Guin graduated from Radcliffe and received a master's degree from Columbia University. In her studies, she became acquainted with the works of Charles Dickens and has noted that his intelligent, responsible female characters have been a strong influence on her own fiction, which she began writing in college. Afterwards, Le Guin moved to Portland, Oregon, where she married and started a family.

So what makes a young mother of three children venture into the intellectual netherworld of science fiction? "It took me years to realize that I chose to work in such despised, marginal genres as science fiction, fantasy, young adult, precisely because they were excluded from critical, academic, canonical supervision, leaving the artist free," she once wrote in *The New York Times Book Review*. "It took ten more years before I had the wits and guts to see and say that the exclusion of the genres from 'literature' is unjustified, unjustifiable, and a matter not of quality but of politics." She made a similar realization about her choice of subjects: until the mid-1970s Le Guin's subjects were "heroic adventures, high-tech futures, men in the halls of power, men—men were the central characters. . . 'Why don't you write about women?' my mother asked me. 'I don't know how,' I said."

Gradually she learned, as the feminist movement inspired deeper exploration of women's lifestyles. From the dispassionate futures depicted in *Planet of Exile* and *Rocannon's World* (both 1966) to *The Lathe of Heaven* (an eerie exploration of a utopian society with domesticated aliens, published in 1971) to *Searoads: The Chronicles of Klatsand* (1991), Le Guin explores possibilities for positive social change. Her taut, rhythm-conscious prose augments her inventive landscapes, challenging new places where women were not restricted by their familiar societal roles. And that's not her only innovation: In *Always Coming Home* (1985), she created a whole new language, complete with glossary.

Always thoughtful, sometimes irreverent, Le Guin's brave new world of writing shows her profound respect for the natural world and its capacity to teach and redeem. Her four *Earthsea* novels, which she began in 1968, are now regarded as classics on the same level as Tolkien's *The Lord of the Rings* trilogy. By daring to invent utopian societies, she has stepped boldly where few women writers have dared to go. "What was and what may be lie," she wrote, "like children whose faces we cannot see, in the arms of silence. All we ever have is here, now."

In this excerpt from The Left Hand of Darkness *(1967), we find the interplanetary diplomat Genly Ai, a human, conversing with Estraven, the prime minister of the planet Gethen. The Gethenians are a race of individuals who are female during some months, and males in others. In this uniquely alien setting, Ai considers his own place.*

I was alone, with a stranger, inside the walls of a dark palace, in a strange snow-changed city, in the heart of the Ice Age of an alien world.

Everything I had said, tonight and ever since I came to Winter, suddenly appeared to me as both stupid and incredible. How could I expect this man or any other to believe my tales about other worlds, other races, a vague benevolent government somewhere off in outer space? It was all nonsense. I had appeared in Karhide in a queer kind of ship, and I differed physically from Gethenians in some respects; that wanted explaining. But my own explanations were preposterous. I did not, in that moment, believe them myself.

"I believe you," said the stranger, the alien alone with me, and so strong had my access of self-alienation been that I looked up at him bewildered. "I'm afraid that Argaven also believes you. But he does not trust you. In part because he no longer trusts me. I have made mistakes, been careless. I cannot ask for your trust any longer, either, having put you in jeopardy. I forgot what a king is, forgot that the king in his own eyes *is* Karhide, forgot what patriotism is and that he is, of necessity, the perfect patriot. Let me ask you this, Mr. Ai: do you know, by your own experience, what patriotism is?"

"No," I said, shaken by the force of that intense personality suddenly turning itself wholly upon me. "I don't think I do. If by patriotism you don't mean the love of one's homeland, for that I do know."

"No, I don't mean love, when I say patriotism. I mean fear. The fear of the other. And its expressions are political, not poetical: hate, rivalry, aggression. It grows in us, that fear. It grows in us year by year. We've followed our road too far. And you, who come from a world that outgrew nations centuries ago, who hardly know what I'm talking about, who show us the new road—" He broke off. After a while he went on, in control again, cool and polite: "It's because of fear that I refuse to urge your cause with the king, now. But not fear for myself, Mr. Ai. I'm not acting patriotically. There are, after all, other nations on Gethen."

I had no idea what he was driving at, but was sure that he did not mean what he seemed to mean. Of all the dark, obstructive, enigmatic souls I had met in this bleak city, his was the darkest. I would not play his labyrinthine game. I made no reply. After a while he went on, rather cautiously, "If I've understood you, your Ekumen is devoted essentially to the general interest of mankind. Now, for instance, the Orgota have experience in subordinating local interests to a general interest, while Karhide has almost none. And the Commensals of Orgoreyn are mostly sane men, if unintelligent, while the king of Karhide is not only insane but rather stupid."

It was clear that Estraven had no loyalties at all. I said in faint disgust, "It must be difficult to serve him, if that's the case."

"I'm not sure I've ever served the king," said the king's prime minister. "Or ever intended to. I'm not anyone's servant. A man must cast his own shadow. . . ."

The gongs in Remny Tower were striking Sixth Hour, midnight, and I took them as my excuse to go. As I was putting on my coat in the hallway he said, "I've lost my chance for the present, for I suppose you'll be leaving Ehrenrang—" why did he suppose so?—"but I trust a day will come when I can ask you questions again. There's so much I want to know. About your mind-speech, in particular; you'd scarcely begun to try to explain it to me."

His curiosity seemed perfectly genuine. He had the effrontery of the powerful. His promises to help me had seemed genuine, too. I said yes, of course, whenever he liked, and that was the evening's end. He showed me out through the garden, where snow lay thin in the light of Gethen's big, dull, rufous moon. I shivered as we went out, for it was well below freezing, and he said with polite surprise, "You're cold?" To him of course it was a mild spring night.

I was tired and downcast. I said, "I've been cold ever since I came to this world."

"What do you call it, this world, in your language?"

"Gethen."

"You gave it no name of your own?"

"Yes, the First Investigators did. They called it Winter."

We had stopped in the gateway of the walled garden. Outside, the Palace grounds and roofs loomed in a dark snowy jumble lit here and there at various heights by the faint gold slits of windows. Standing under the narrow arch I glanced up, wondering if that keystone too was mortared with bone and blood. Estraven took leave of me and turned away; he was never fulsome in his greetings and farewells. I went off through the silent courts and alleys of the Palace, my boots crunching on the thin moonlit snow, and homeward through the deep streets of the city. I was cold, unconfident, obsessed by perfidy, and solitude, and fear.

Toni Morrison

(born 1931)

Admirers have likened Toni Morrison's talent for conjuring music from the everyday speech of African Americans to a sort of black magic. The comparison is not lost on Morrison, one of the most significant contemporary voices in American literature. "We were intimate with the supernatural," she says of her family's easy belief in the otherworld. That belief has resulted in the rich mysticism that permeates her fiction.

Morrison is the second of four children. She was born Chloe Anthony Wofford, to migrant workers who left the South for a better life across the Mason-Dixon line. Her grandparents were sharecroppers in Georgia. Her work draws upon her family's experiences in the South, as well as her own childhood memories of Lorain, Ohio, which she describes as "a neighborhood, a life-giving and sustaining compound, a village in the traditional African sense, where myth abounds." Such a town provides the setting for Morrison's first novel, *The Bluest Eye* (1970), an unsentimental story about Pecola, a young black girl caught up in a downward spiral of family tragedy.

Despite precocity as a student of literature, Morrison came to fiction writing fairly late in life. A Latin scholar at Lorain High School, she graduated with honors and went on to study the classics at Howard University, where she received an English degree in 1953. After obtaining a masters in the same discipline at Cornell University in 1955, she returned to Howard to teach English. It wasn't until she had married, borne two sons, divorced, and taken a position as an editor of black fiction at Random House in New York that she discovered fiction writing as a path to self-expression.

Following *The Bluest Eye*, Morrison strode this path with an impressive gait. *Sula* (1974), a novel about the steamy, symbiotic friendship between two women, earned her a

Toni Morrison

National Book Award nomination. *Song of Solomon* (1977), loosely based on her grandfather's search for his heritage, won two literary awards. But it was *Tar Baby* (1981), a daring examination of the doomed romance between an Americanized black woman and her Rastafarian lover, that landed the author on the cover of *Newsweek* and placed Morrison in the mainstream of American literature. Her position was cemented with the publication of *Beloved* (1987), an extraordinary examination of the physical and psychological effects of slavery on a former slave and her lover, for which she was awarded the Pulitzer Prize for fiction.

Morrison followed this achievement with the novel *Jazz* (1992) and the study *Playing in the Dark: Whiteness and the Literary Imagination* (1992). That year she also edited *Race-ing Justice, Engender-ing Power: Essays on Anita Hill, Clarence Thomas and the Construction of Social Reality*. Its mission seems to recall a thought from her very first novel. In the preface to *The Bluest Eye*, when Pecola's dismal end is foreshadowed, Morrison writes, "There is really nothing more to say—except why. But since why is difficult to handle, we must take refuge in how."

In 1993, Morrison received the Nobel Prize for Literature. According to a statement issued by the Nobel Committee of the Swedish Academy, Morrison won the most powerful award in the world because "She delves into the language itself, a language she wants to liberate from the fetters of race. And she addresses us with the luster of poetry."

Pilate is a sort of good witch, a pivotal character in Song of Solomon *(1977). Morrison's novel follows the search of a man, who goes by his childhood name Milkman, toward the resolution of certain mysteries of his youth. Here, the author explains what makes Pilate so special—aside from the fact that she's treated as an object of suspicion because she was born without a navel.*

It isolated her. Already without family, she was further isolated from her people, for, except for the relative bliss on the island, every other resource was denied her: partnership in marriage, confessional friendship, and communal religion. Men frowned, women whispered and shoved their children behind them. Even a traveling side show would have rejected her, since her freak quality lacked that important ingredient—the grotesque. There was really nothing to see. Her defect, frightening and exotic as it was, was also a theatrical failure. It needed intimacy, gossip, and the time it took for curiosity to become drama.

Finally Pilate began to take offense. Although she was hampered by huge ignorances, but not in any way unintelligent, when she realized what her situation in the world was and would probably always be she threw away every assumption she had learned and began at zero. First off, she cut her hair. That was one thing she didn't want to have to think about anymore. Then she tackled the problem of trying to decide how she wanted to live and what was valuable to her. When am I happy and when am I sad and what is the difference? What do I need to know to stay alive? What is true in the world? Her mind traveled crooked streets and aimless goat paths, arriving sometimes at profundity, other times at the revelations of a three-year-old. Throughout this fresh, if common, pursuit of knowledge, one conviction crowned her efforts: since death held no terrors for her (she spoke often to the dead), she knew there was nothing to fear. That plus her alien's compassion for troubled people ripened her and—the consequence of the knowledge she had made up or acquired—kept her just barely within the boundaries of the elaborately socialized world of black people. Her dress might be outrageous to them, but her respect for other people's privacy—which they were all very intense about—was balancing. She stared at people, and in those days looking straight into another person's eyes was considered among black people the height of rudeness, an act acceptable only with and among children and certain kinds of outlaws—but she never made an impolite observation. And true to the palm oil that flowed in her veins, she never had a visitor to whom she did not offer food before one word of conversation—business or social—began. She laughed but never smiled and in 1963, when she was sixty-eight years old, she had not shed a tear since Circe had brought her cherry jam for breakfast.

She gave up, apparently, all interest in table manners or hygiene, but acquired a deep concern for and about human relationships. Those twelve years in Montour County, where she had been treated gently by a father and a brother, and where she herself was in a position to help farm animals under her care, had taught her a preferable kind of behavior. Preferable to that of the men who called her mermaid and the women who swept up her footprints or put mirrors on her door.

She was a natural healer, and among quarreling drunks and fighting women she could hold her own, and sometimes mediated a peace that lasted a good bit longer than it should have because it was administered by someone not like them. But most important, she paid close attention to her mentor—the father who appeared before her sometimes and told her things. After Reba was born, he no longer came to Pilate dressed as he had been on the woods' edge and in the cave, when she and Macon had left Circe's house. Then he had worn the coveralls and heavy shoes he was shot in. Now he came in a white shirt, a blue collar, and a brown peaked cap. He wore no shoes (they were tied together and slung over his shoulder), probably because his feet hurt, since he rubbed his toes a lot as he sat near her bed or on the porch, or rested against the side of the still. Along with winemaking, cooking whiskey became the way Pilate began to make her steady living. That skill allowed her more freedom hour by hour and day by day than any other work a woman of no means whatsoever and no inclination to make love for money could choose. Once settled in as a small-time bootlegger in the colored section of a town, she had only occasional police or sheriff problems, for she allowed none of the activities that often accompanied wine houses—women, gambling—and she more often that not refused to let her customers drink what they bought from her on the premises. She made and sold liquor. Period.

After Reba grew up and began to live from one

orgasm to another, taking time out to produce one child, Hagar, Pilate thought it might be time for a change. Not because of Reba, who was quite content with the life her mother and she lived, but because of her granddaughter. Hagar was prissy. She hated, even as a two-year-old, dirt and disorganization. At three she was already vain and beginning to be proud. She liked pretty clothes. Astonished as Pilate and Reba were by her wishes, they enjoyed trying to fulfill them. They spoiled her, and she, as a favor to their indulgence, hid as best she could the fact that they embarrassed her.

Pilate decided to find her brother, if he was still alive, for the child, Hagar, needed family, people, a life very different from what she and Reba could offer, and if she remembered anything about Macon, he would be different. Prosperous, conventional, more like the things and people Hagar seemed to admire. In addition, Pilate wanted to make peace between them. She asked her father where he was, but he just rubbed his feet and shook his head. So for the first time, Pilate went voluntarily to the police, who sent her to the Red Cross, who sent her to the Salvation Army, who sent her to the Society of Friends, who sent her back to the Salvation Army, who wrote to their command posts in large cities from New York to St. Louis and from Detroit to Louisiana and asked them to look in the telephone directory, where in fact one captain's secretary found him listed. Pilate was surprised that they were successful, but the captain was not, because there could hardly be many people with such a name.

They made the trip in style (one train and two buses), for Pilate had a lot of money; the crash of 1929 had produced so many buyers of cheap home brew she didn't even need the collection the Salvation Army took up for her. She arrived with suitcases, a green sack, a full-grown daughter, and a grand-daughter, and found her brother truculent, inhospitable, embarrassed, and unforgiving. Pilate would have moved on immediately except for her brother's wife, who was dying of lovelessness then, and seemed to be dying of it now as she sat at the table across from her sister-in-law listening to her life story, which Pilate was making deliberately long to keep Ruth's mind off Hagar.

Edna O'Brien

(born 1932)

Edna O'Brien is not afraid to speak the truth. Her first novel, *The Country Girls* (1960), was considered scandalous for its frank descriptions of female independence and sexual awakenings. Even worse, O'Brien admitted that this story of Kate Brady and Baba Brennan, who escape their quiet country homes and strict convent school for the big city of Dublin, was autobiographical in nature. The schoolgirls were out to have the sort of lusty adventure usually reserved in literature for young men.

Like Kate and Baba, O'Brien was born in County Clare in western Ireland. The women of her tiny rural town escaped the doldrums of the place by reading dime novels and sharing romantic classics like *Gone with the Wind*. O'Brien attended a convent school and, at age fourteen, went to live in Dublin. There she worked in a chemist shop by day and attended university lectures at night. Discovering the works of James Joyce, she began writing and submitting her work to the *Irish Press*. In 1952 she eloped with Ernest Gebler, a writer. In 1959 O'Brien moved to London with her two sons and worked for a publisher, who encouraged her to write. She produced *The Country Girls* in just three weeks.

The forthrightness of that book—Ireland's version of *Peyton Place*—in her conservative, largely Catholic homeland of Ireland brought O'Brien profound notoriety. Like many modern Irish writers, including Joyce and the playwright Sean O'Casey, her work was banned in Ireland under the Censorship of Publications Act of 1929, which prohibited the publication of work considered "indecent or obscene" or which advocates birth control. Virtually everything she published during the 1960s, including two sequels to her first novel, *The Lonely Girl* (1962) and *Girls in Their Married Bliss* (1963) was banned by the Irish

Edna O'Brien

government. As a result, she became one of the few writers of her generation to openly protest censorship. In 1964, she divorced her husband.

O'Brien eventually turned her clear, truthful gaze to subjects other than those who resembled herself, though virtually all of her protagonists have been women. Many of her characters are based on the inhabitants of tiny Irish villages, their lives consumed with small-town gossip and fervent (albeit judgmental) Catholicism. Priests and nuns, neighborhood eccentrics, family members involved in tangled, ambivalent relationships— O'Brien's portraits of them through the years have been unfailingly eloquent and intelligent.

Her literary output has been prolific: five screenplays, including *Three into Two Won't Go* (1969), and two stage plays, one about the life of Virginia Woolf (1980). O'Brien has also continued publishing novels and short story collections, among them *August Is a Wicked Month* (1964); *The Love Object* (1968); *A Pagan Place* (1971); *Johnny I hardly knew you* (1977); and *A Fanatic Heart: Selected Stories* (1985). In the United States, her pieces have appeared frequently in *The New Yorker*, as well as in women's magazines such as *Redbook*. O'Brien's most recent book is the short-story collection *Lantern Slides* (1991). She currently lives in London, still telling her truth.

In this early scene from O'Brien's semi-autobiographical novel The Country Girls, *the character Kate suffers the confines of the strict convent school she longs to leave.*

That first evening in the chapel was strange and emotional. The incense floated down the nave, followed by the articulate voice of the priest, who knelt before the altar in a gold-crusted cloak.

We knelt in the back of the chapel on wooden benches, and there were wooden rails separating us from where the nuns knelt. The nuns were one in front of the other in little oak compartments that were fixed to the walls on either side. They all looked alike from the back except the postulants, who wore lace bonnets and whose hair showed through the lace.

We all filed out of the chapel, making as much noise as twenty horses galloping over a stony road. Some girls had studs in their shoes and you could hear the studs scratching the tile floor of the chapel porch. We went down to the recreation hall, where Sister Margaret was sitting on a rostrum, waiting to speak to us. She welcomed the new girls, rewelcomed the old ones, and gave a quick summary of the convent rules:

Silence in the dormitory, and at breakfast.
Shoes to be taken off before going into the dormitory.
No food to be kept in presses in the dormitory.
To bed within twenty minutes after you go upstairs.

"Now," she said, "will the girls who wish to have milk at night please put up their hands?" I had a bad chest, so I put up my hand and committed myself to a lukewarm cup of dusty milk every night; and committed my father to a bill for two pounds a year.

Scholarships did not cater to bad chests.

We went to bed early.

Our dormitory was on the first floor. There was a lavatory on the landing outside it, and twenty or thirty girls were queueing there, hopping from one foot to another as if they couldn't wait. I took off my shoes and carried them into the dormitory. It was a long room with windows on either side, and a door at the far end. Over the door was a large crucifix, and there were holy pictures along the yellow distempered walls. There were two rows of iron beds down the length of the room. They were covered with white cotton counterpanes, and the iron was painted white as well. The beds were numbered and I found mine easily enough. Baba was six beds away from me. At least it was nice to know that she was near, in case we should ever speak. There were three radiators along the wall, but they were cold.

I sat down on the chair beside my bed, took off my garters, and peeled my stockings off slowly. The garters were too tight and they had made marks on my legs. I was looking at the red marks, worrying in case I'd have varicose veins before morning, and I didn't know that Sister Margaret was standing right behind me. She wore rubber-soled shoes and she had a way of stealing up on one. I jumped off the chair when she said, "Now, girls." I turned around to face her. Her eyes were cross and I could see a small cyst on one of her irises. She was that near to me.

"The new girls won't know this, but our convent has always been proud of its modesty. Our girls, above anything else, are good and wholesome and modest. One expression of modesty is the way a girl dresses and undresses. She should do so with decorum and modesty. In an open dormitory like this . . ." She paused, because someone had come in the bottom door and had bashed a ewer against the woodwork. Even my earlobes were blushing. She went on: "Upstairs the senior girls have separate cubicles; but, as I say, in an open dormitory like this, girls are requested to dress and undress under the shelter of their dressing gowns. Girls should face the foot of the bed doing this, as they might surprise each other if they face the side of the bed." She coughed and went off twiddling a bunch of keys in the air. She unlocked the oak door at the end of the room and went out.

The girl allotted to the bed next to mine raised her eyes to heaven. She had squint eyes and I didn't like her. Not because of the squint, but because she looked like someone who would have bad taste about everything. She was wearing a pretty, expensive dressing gown and rich fluffy slippers; but you felt that she bought them to show off, and not because they were pretty. I saw her put two bars of chocolate under her pillow.

Trying to undress under a dressing gown is a talent you must develop. Mine fell off six or seven times, but finally I managed to keep it on by stooping very low.

I was rooting in my travel bag when the lights went out. Small figures in nightgowns hurried up the carpeted passage and disappeared into the cold white beds.

I wanted to get the cake that was in the bottom of my bag. The tea service was on top, so I took it out piece by piece. Baba crept up to the foot of my bed, and for the first time we talked, or rather, we whispered.

"Jesus, 'tis hell," she said. "I won't stick it for a week."

"Nor me. Are you hungry?"

"I'd eat a young child," she said. I was just getting my nail file out of my toilet bag, to cut a hunk of cake with, when the key was turned in the door at the end of the room. I covered the cake quickly with a towel and we stood there perfectly still, as Sister Margaret came toward us, holding her flashlight.

"What is the meaning of this?" she asked. She knew our names already and addressed us by our full names, not just Bridget (Baba's real name) and Caithleen, but Bridget Brennan and Caithleen Brady.

"We were lonely, Sister," I said.

"You are not alone in your loneliness. Loneliness is no excuse for disobedience." She was speaking in a penetrating whisper. The whole dormitory could hear her.

"Go back to your bed, Bridget Brennan," she said. Baba tripped off quietly. Sister Margaret shone the flashlight to and fro, until the beam caught the little tea service on the bed.

"What is this?" she asked, picking up one of the cups.

"A tea service, Sister. I brought it because my mother died." It was a stupid thing to say and I regretted it at once. I'm always saying stupid things, because I don't think before I say them.

"Sentimental childish conduct," she said. She lifted the outside layer of her black habit and shaped it into a basket. Then she put the tea service in there and carried it off.

I got in between the icy sheets and ate a piece of seed cake. The whole dormitory was crying. You could hear the sobbing and choking under the covers. Smothered crying.

The head of my bed backed onto the head of another girl's bed, and in the dark a hand came through the rungs and put a bun on my pillow. It was an iced bun and there was something on top of the icing. Possibly a cherry. I gave her a piece of cake and we shook hands. I wondered what she looked like, as I hadn't noticed her when the lights were on. She was a nice girl, whoever she was. The bun was nice, too. Two or three beds away I heard some girl munch an apple under the covers. Everyone seemed to be eating and crying for their mothers.

My bed faced a window and I could see a sprinkling of stars in one small corner of the sky. It was nice to lie there watching the stars, waiting for them to fade or to go out, or to flare up into one brilliant firework. Waiting for something to happen in the deathly, unhappy silence.

George Sand

(1804–1876)

"The mind has no sex," observed the most famous female writer of nineteenth-century France. Perhaps George Sand's controversial views about love, marriage, and equality for women explain why her works fell into oblivion after her death, despite their critical acclaim when published. Author of more than sixty novels, plays, stories, essays, memoirs, and an astounding forty thousand letters, Sand became better known for wearing men's clothes, smoking in public, and taking lovers than for her thoughtful, opinionated writing. It was only during the late 1960s that feminist scholars began to rediscover her books.

George Sand was born Amantine Aurore Lucile Dupin in Paris. Her father was an army officer, and the family moved frequently when she was a child. The Dupins eventually settled in Nohant in central France. After attending a convent school in Paris, Aurore, as she was called, returned to the sleepy countryside of Nohant.

At 18, she married Baron Casimir Dudevant, and had two children. The baron was abusive, and in 1830, Aurore fled to Paris. Determined to earn enough money to send for her children, she began to write. Her first novel concerned two convent girls named in the title, *Rose et Blanche* (1831). She collaborated on it with a lover, Jules Sandeau, and it was published under the name J. Sand. Soon, Aurore received an offer to write for a major political journal. Meanwhile, wishing to attend the theater and sit in less expensive seats prohibited to women, she began wearing men's clothes, and was pleased by the anonymity they afforded her.

In 1832, hoping to capitalize on the success of *Rose et Blanche* while establishing her

George Sand

own pseudonym, she wrote *Indiana* under the name George Sand. In this tale of a woman in a loveless marriage, Sand expressed her opinion that monogamy was abnormal. *Indiana* brought her great notoriety, as did *Valentine* (1832) and *Lelia* (1833), passionate explorations of women's desire for freedom and sexual satisfaction. She became the toast of Paris and scandalized society by taking a series of high-profile lovers, including Frederic Chopin.

In the late 1830s and 40s, a time of great upheaval in Napoleonic France, Sand became a nonviolent political activist, writing pamphlets advocating the overthrow of the monarchy. She grew interested in mystical Christianity, and wrote plays, essays, children's stories, and novels, including *Fanchon the Cricket* (1847). This, along with her 1854 autobiography *Histoire de Ma Vie (Story of My Life)*, and letters she exchanged with writer Gustave Flaubert, are Sand's best known works. Her last book, *Marianne* (1876), concerns an independent young woman who takes up with an older man. She set the novel in Nohant, 50 years in the past, when the extraordinary circumstances of her own life away from that quiet place in the French countryside were just beginning.

An attractive, independenty minded female character who questions the institution of marriage was something of an anomaly in nineteenth century France, as illustrated in this passage from Sand's charming novel Marianne.

Marianne's features were very delicate and her teeth very beautiful. All she needed to be really pretty was to believe herself so.

"Well now," said Madame André, embracing her. "We know what's brought our little darling to us tonight. So you've decided to get married!"

"No, Madame André," replied Marianne, "I have decided nothing, yet."

"Ah, but, . . . since you've decided to receive a suitor, it follows you'll accept him if he suits you."

"Well, that's the whole question. For the moment, I'm just looking, as they say. Are you willing to bring him over to me on Sunday?"

"Certainly, my dear, I could never refuse you anything."

"I'll leave you two in peace to discuss this weighty problem," said Pierre André, making for the meadow. "On this interesting topic, women always have little secrets they want to confide in each other. I should be in your way."

"Oh, no," said Marianne. "There are absolutely no secrets between us and I refuse to think about the idea until both you and your mother have told me what I should do about this person."

"What! You mean you would listen to what we thought before you decided?"

"Certainly."

"I cannot accept any such responsibility," replied André drily. "I'm no connoisseur of husbands and I think you're making fun of us, playing the innocent like this."

"How could I be anything but innocent?" said Marianne, her eyes opening wide in astonishment.

"Well, you know why you rejected the others so you must know what you want and why you might accept this one!"

"Him, or someone else!" replied Marianne smiling. "Don't go away, please. I've got something to ask you."

"Oh, *really!* That's too much! Now you want to know what sort of husband you should choose, do you?"

The three sat down on a bench, with Madame André in the middle.

"No," replied Marianne. "You couldn't tell me that. You couldn't give me a serious answer because you're not very interested in my future. No, I'd like to ask you something which is only indirectly related to the question of marriage. I should like to know whether a girl in my position can educate herself without leaving her home and her accustomed ways."

"What a very singular question she's putting to me," said Pierre to his mother. "Can you make head or tail of it?"

"But of course I can," replied Madame André. "And this isn't the first time Marianne has racked her brains over the problem. I am in no position to give her advice myself. All I've learned is what I was taught as a young girl. That is all that's necessary for a poor country housewife like myself. But it doesn't take you very far. There are many topics I never bring up because I don't understand the first thing about them. The wisest thing a woman in my situation can do is not to ask questions for fear of showing her own ignorance. But that's not good enough for Marianne. She doesn't want simply to learn tact and diplomacy; she would like to be able to talk about all sorts of things with educated people."

"Forgive me, Madame André," said Marianne, "but I should like to be educated not so much for others' pleasure as for my own. I see for example that my godfather is happy walking about alone for days on end, thinking about all he knows. I'd like to know if he is happier than I, who go for the same long walks but without knowing anything and without thinking about anything."

Charlotte Brontë

(1816–1855)

One of the best-loved English writers of the nineteenth century, Charlotte Brontë had a gift for creating fictional relationships between men and women that still capture our emotions. Imagine how surprised she would be to learn that both her work and that of her sister Emily had become the stuff of Hollywood movies and Broadway shows!

Charlotte was raised in Yorkshire, England. Her mother died when Charlotte was very young. Her father, a minister, spent a great deal of time reading with his children. Isolated in a parsonage on the lonely Yorkshire moors, the Brontë siblings—Charlotte, Anne, Emily, and Branwell—created fictional empires based on Branwell's toy soldiers. Perhaps inevitably, all became writers. But it is Charlotte who achieved the greatest recognition for her novels *Shirley*, *Villette*, and *Jane Eyre*.

After briefly attending local schools, Charlotte tutored her sisters and worked nearby as a governess. In 1842, she and Emily traveled to Brussels to study French. Charlotte remained in Belgium for a year to study and teach English. The Brontës' literary careers began when they co-authored a pseudonymous collection, *Poems by Currer, Ellis, and Acton Bell* (1846). Charlotte's first novel, *The Professor*, was rejected by several London publishers. But soon all three sisters rejoiced in each other's successes when *Jane Eyre*, *Wuthering Heights*, and *Agnes Grey* were published in 1847. Their joy was short-lived, however, for Anne, Emily, and Branwell died within a year of one another—the sisters of tuberculosis and their brother of alcohol and possibly drug addiction.

Charlotte, meanwhile, had joined London's literary elite. She befriended

Charlotte Brontë

William Makepeace Thackeray and Elizabeth Gaskell, the latter of whom became her first posthumous biographer. With the success of *Jane Eyre*, wrote Gaskell, "Henceforward Charlotte Brontë's existence [became] divided into two parallel currents—her life as Currer Bell, the author; her life as Charlotte Brontë, the woman." The literary life presented a conflict between the traditional role of women in the Victorian era, and the allure of work and fame.

Jane Eyre, one of the greatest works of English fiction, met with instant acclaim. The epic tale of love between the governess Jane and the wealthy Mr. Rochester is written with a frankness unusual for conservative Victorian times. Charlotte's second novel, *Shirley* (1849), concerns the struggles of two women from different social classes.

It was followed by *Villette* (1853), the story of a young teacher's attraction to a handsome doctor. The following year, Charlotte married A. B. Nicholls, a Haworth curate. By most reports, she did not love him, but their union was destined to be brief, for she died eight months later of pneumonia. Her children's stories, many based on the fantasy kingdom she created with her siblings, were published posthumously.

The governess Jane Eyre is forthright, strong, and unashamed of her emotions when, in the throes of a violent thunderstorm, Mr. Rochester declares his love and asks her to marry him. He may be her employer, but she is every bit his equal.

"Do you doubt me, Jane?"

"Entirely."

"You have no faith in me?"

"Not a whit."

"Am I a liar in your eyes?" he asked passionately. "Little sceptic, you *shall* be convinced. What love have I for Miss Ingram? None: and that you know. What love has she for me? None: as I have taken pains to prove: I caused a rumour to reach her that my fortune was not a third of what was supposed, and after that I presented myself to see the result; it was coldness both from her and her mother. I would not—I could not—marry Miss Ingram. You—you strange, you almost unearthly thing!—I love you as my own flesh. You—poor and obscure, and small and plain as you are—I entreat to accept me as a husband."

"What, me!" I ejaculated, beginning in his earnestness especially in his incivility—to credit his sincerity: "me who have not a friend in the world but you—if you are my friend: not a shilling but what you have given me?"

"You, Jane, I must have you for my own—entirely my own. Will you be mine? Say yes, quickly."

"Mr. Rochester, let me look at your face: turn to the moonlight."

"Why?"

"Because I want to read your countenance—turn!"

"There! you will find it scarcely more legible than a crumpled, scratched page. Read on: only make haste, for I suffer."

His face was very much agitated and very much flushed, and there were strong workings in the features, and strange gleams in the eyes.

"Oh, Jane, you torture me!" he exclaimed. "With that searching and yet faithful and generous look, you torture me!"

"How can I do that? If you are true, and your offer real, my only feelings to you must be gratitude and devotion—they cannot torture."

"Gratitude!" he ejaculated; and added wildly—"Jane, accept me quickly. Say, Edward—give me my name—Edward—I will marry you."

"Are you in earnest? Do you truly love me? Do you sincerely wish me to be your wife?"

"I do; and if an oath is necessary to satisfy, I swear it."

"Then, sir, I will marry you."

"Edward—my little wife!"

"Dear Edward!"

"Come to me—come to me entirely now," said he, and added in his deepest tone, speaking in my ear as his cheek was laid on mine, "Make my happiness—I will make yours."

"God pardon me!" he subjoined ere long; "and man meddle not with me: I have her, and will hold her."

"There is no one to meddle, sir. I have no kindred to interfere."

"No—that is the best of it," he said. And if I had loved him less I should have thought his accent and look of exultation savage; but, sitting by him, roused from the nightmare of parting—called to the paradise of union—I thought only of the bliss given me to drink in so abundant a flow. Again and again he said, "Are you happy, Jane?" And again and again I answered, "Yes." After which he murmured, "It will atone—it will atone. Have I not found her friendless, and cold, and comfortless? Will I not guard, and cherish, and solace her? Is there not love in my heart, and constancy in my resolves? It will expiate at God's tribunal. I know my Maker sanctions what I do. For the world's judgement—I wash my hands thereof. For man's opinion—I defy it."

But what had befallen the night? The moon was not yet set, and we were all in shadow: I could scarcely see my master's face, near as I was. And what ailed the chestnut tree? it writhed and groaned; while wind roared in the laurel walk, and came sweeping over us.

"We must go in," said Mr. Rochester: "the weather changes. I could have sat with thee till morning, Jane."

"And so," thought I, "could I with you." I should have said so, perhaps, but a livid, vivid spark leapt out of a cloud at which I was looking, and there was a crack, a crash, and a dose rattling peal; and I thought only of hiding my dazzled eyes against Mr. Rochester's shoulder. The rain rushed down. He hurried me up the walk, through the grounds, and into the house; but we were quite wet before we could pass the threshold. He was taking off my shawl in the hall, and shaking the water out of my loosened hair, when Mrs. Fairfax emerged from her room. I did not observe her at first, nor did Mr. Rochester. The lamp was lit. The clock was on the stroke of twelve.

"Hasten to take off your wet things," said he; "and before you go, good-night—good-night, my darling."

He kissed me repeatedly. When I looked up, on leaving his arms, there stood the widow, pale, grave, and amazed. I only smiled at her, and ran upstairs. "Explanation will do for another time," thought I. Still, when I reached my chamber, I felt a pang at the idea she should even temporarily misconstrue what she had seen. But joy soon effaced every other feeling; and loud as the wind blew, near and deep as the thunder crashed, fierce and frequent as the lightning gleamed, cataract-like as the rain fell during a storm of two hours' duration, I experienced no fear and little awe. Mr. Rochester came thrice to my door in the course of it, to ask if I was safe and tranquil: and that was comfort that was strength for anything.

Before I left my bed in the morning, little Adèle came running in to tell me that the great horse-chest-nut at the bottom of the orchard had been struck by lightning in the night, and half of it split away.

Christina Rossetti

(1830–1894)

A major poet of Victorian England, Christina Rossetti wrote about passion and loss with an intensity that belied the staid circumstances of her life. She was born in London to Italian parents. As a child, she played in the countryside, enjoying nature and robust health. But in adolescence, confined to a big house in the city, she was often ill and depressed, conditions which were to plague her all her life. This dichotomy between the forces that shaped Rossetti's life became a theme in her writing, as did her strong religious beliefs as a High Anglican.

Christina's father was a poet and professor of Italian. Her mother, who had been a governess, educated Christina at home. Her grandfather, who had his own printing press, produced Christina's first book of verse in 1842. Dante Gabriel Rossetti, her brother and a major poet in his own right, became a founding member of the Pre-Raphaelite Brotherhood, a movement of painters and writers opposed to what they believed was a stagnation in contemporary art. Christina contributed poetry, under a pseudonym, to their magazine, *The Germ*. She also posed as a model for several Pre-Raphaelite artists, including her brother, who painted her in his 1849 *The Girlhood of Mary Virgin*.

When James Collinson, a Pre-Raphaelite and a Roman Catholic, proposed to Christina in 1848, she initially accepted, then broke the engagement, citing the difference in their religious beliefs. She rejected another suitor for the same reason. Rossetti never married, although the melancholy of lost love was an emotion often expressed in her work. Her career took off with publication of three poems, under her own name, in *MacMillan's*

Magazine. Among her best known is "Up-hill." It recounts a metaphorical ascent up a difficult road, with reward—i.e. religious salvation—at the end. The book *Goblin Market and Other Poems* (1862) established her reputation as a major writer. The lengthy title poem is an allegory about two sisters tempted by forbidden fruit, and their differing reactions to the terrible goblins who offer it. In its evocation of fear and lust, the poem illustrates Rossetti's internal struggle between passion and denial.

In her fifties, Christina was afflicted with a thyroid disorder, and rarely left home, although she continued to write. Her subjects ranged from politics to poverty and illegitimate children, no doubt as a result of her work at a shelter for unwed mothers and prostitutes. Later works include *A Pageant and Other Poems* (1881), and *The Face of the Deep* (1892). Increasingly ill, Christina lived the last fifteen years of her life as a virtual recluse. While under consideration as England's next poet laureate, following Alfred Lord Tennyson, she died of cancer at the age of sixty-four.

In this excerpt from "The Goblin Market," her complex and wildly evocative poem about two sisters, Rossetti describes the sad results of yielding to temptation. Literary critics have attributed the poem's allegorical nature to the poet's own dedication to Christianity.

Early in the morning
When the first cock crowed his warning,
Neat like bees, as sweet and busy,
Laura rose with Lizzie:
Fetched in honey, milked the cows,
Aired and set to rights the house,
Kneaded cakes of whitest wheat,
Cakes for dainty mouths to eat,
Next churned butter, whipped up cream,
Fed their poultry, sat and sewed;
Talked as modest maidens should:
Lizzie with an open heart,
Laura in an absent dream,
One content, one sick in part;
One warbling for the mere bright day's
   delight,

One longing for the night.
At length slow evening came:
They went with pitchers to the reedy brook;
Lizzie most placid in her look,
Laura most like a leaping flame.
They drew the gurgling water from its deep;
Lizzie plucked purple and rich golden flags,
Then turning homewards said: "The sunset
   flushes
Those furthest loftiest crags;
Come, Laura, not another maiden lags,
No wilful squirrel wags,
The beasts and birds are fast asleep."
But Laura loitered still among the rushes
And said the bank was steep.
And said the hour was early still,

Christina Rossetti

The dew not fall'n, the wind not chill:
Listening ever, but not catching
The customary cry,
"Come buy, come buy,"
With its iterated jingle
Of sugar-baited words:
Not for all her watching
Once discerning even one goblin
Racing, whisking, tumbling, hobbling;
Let alone the herds
That used to tramp along the glen,
In groups or single,
Of brisk fruit-merchant men.
Till Lizzie urged, "O Laura, come;
I hear the fruit-call but I dare not look:
You should not loiter longer at this brook:
Come with me home.
The stars rise, the moon bends her arc,
Each glowworm winks her spark,
Let us get home before the night grows dark:
For clouds may gather
Tho' this is summer weather,
Put out the lights and drench us thro';
Then if we lost our way what should we do?"
Laura turned cold as stone
To find her sister heard that cry alone,
That goblin cry, "Come buy our fruits, come
   buy."

Must she then buy no more such dainty fruit?
Must she no more such succous pasture find,
Gone deaf and blind?
Her tree of life drooped from the root:
She said not one word in her heart's sore ache;
But peering thro' the dimness, nought
   discerning,
Trudged home, her pitcher dripping all the
   way;
So crept to bed, and lay
Silent till Lizzie slept;
Then sat up in a passionate yearning,
And gnashed her teeth for baulked desire,
   and wept
As if her heart would break.
Day after day, night after night,
Laura kept watch in vain
In sullen silence of exceeding pain.
She never caught again the goblin cry:
"Come buy, come buy;"—
She never spied the goblin men
Hawking their fruits along the glen:
But when the noon waxed bright
Her hair grew thin and gray;
She dwindled, as the fair full moon cloth
   turn
To swift decay and burn
Her fire away.

Pearl S. Buck

(1892–1973)

The only woman to receive both Nobel and Pulitzer prizes, Pearl Comfort Sydenstricker Buck was born in West Virginia and brought to China when she was three months old. Her parents were missionaries based in Chinkiang, on the Yangtze River, and she was educated primarily at home by her mother and a Chinese tutor. She briefly attended school in Shanghai, a large, culturally advanced city with a substantial international population.

Growing up bilingual in China shaped Pearl's outlook on life. She lamented the then-common practice of female infanticide, reveled in folk legends of female warriors who vanquished dragons, and observed first-hand the devastation of the Boxer Rebellion, a 1900 uprising by Chinese nationalists. As a result of her experiences, she developed a profound sense of responsibility to the poor and disenfranchised. She grew up to become one of the world's great humanitarians, a pioneering advocate for international adoption, children's welfare, civil rights, women's rights, and social services for the mentally handicapped.

In 1910, Pearl returned to America to attend Randolph-Macon Woman's College in Virginia. She went back to China after graduation and married John Lossing Buck, an agricultural economist. They lived in Anwei, a rural province where peasants struggled to make a living from the land. The culture Pearl observed there inspired her to write essays and stories for magazines, as well as her first book, *East Wind, West Wind*, and the Pulitzer Prize-winning *The Good Earth*. In 1921, she gave birth to a retarded daughter. Four years later, she and Buck adopted a baby girl. After the marriage broke up, Pearl married Richard Walsh, her book publisher.

When China experienced political unrest in the early 1930s, Pearl and her family moved to Bucks County, Pennsylvania, and she adopted six more children. She established Welcome House, a pioneering adoption agency that placed Asian and Amerasian children, formerly considered unadoptable, as well as the Pearl S. Buck Foundation, dedicated to caring for mentally retarded children. Somehow, she found time to write nearly 80 books: novels, essays, nonfiction, poetry, and children's stories. *The Good Earth* remains a modern classic, set against the background of China's turbulent twentieth-century history. For most Westerners, it provided the first sympathetic, realistic portrait of the Chinese, in contrast to prevailing stereotypes. The book is part of a trilogy, along with *Sons* (1932) and *A House Divided* (1935).

Not all of Buck's works received critical acclaim, and literary experts generally rank the *House of Earth* trilogy and her other "China books"—*The Mother* (1933), *Dragon Seed* (1938), *Kinfolk* (1949), *Imperial Woman* (1956)—as her finest, along with the autobiography *My Several Worlds* (1954). She died in Bucks County at eighty.

In this vivid excerpt from The Good Earth *(1931), Wang Lung and O-lan, who are starving after a drought ruins the crops, leave their farm to join a growing community of destitute peasants who just barely eke out an existence in the city.*

Day by day beneath the opulence of this city Wang Lung lived in the foundations of poverty upon which it was laid. With the food spilling out of the markets, with the streets of the silk shops flying brilliant banners of black and red and orange silk to announce their wares, with rich men clothed in satin and in velvet, soft-fleshed rich men with their skin covered with garments of silk and their hands like flowers for softness and perfume and the beauty of idleness, with all of these for the regal beauty of the city, in that part where Wang Lung lived there was not food enough to feed savage hunger and not clothes enough to cover bones.

Men labored all day at the baking of breads and cakes for feasts for the rich and children labored from dawn to midnight and slept all greasy and grimed as they were upon rough pallets on the floor and staggered to the ovens next day, and there was not money enough given them to buy a piece of the rich breads they made for others. And men and women labored at the cutting and contriving of heavy furs for the winter and of soft light furs for the spring and at the thick brocaded silks, to cut and shape them into sumptuous robes for the ones who ate of the profusion at the markets, and they themselves snatched a bit of coarse blue cotton cloth and sewed it hastily together to cover their bareness.

Wang Lung living among these who labored at feasting others, heard strange things of which he took little heed. The older men and women, it is true, said nothing to anyone. Greybeards pulled rickshas, pushed wheelbarrows of coal and wood to bakeries and palaces, strained their backs until the muscles stood forth like ropes and they pushed and pulled the heavy carts of merchandise over the cobbled roads, ate frugally of their scanty food, slept their brief nights

Pearl S. Buck

out, and were silent. Their faces were like the face of O-lan; inarticulate, dumb. None knew what was in their minds. If they spoke at all it was of food or of pence. Rarely was the word silver upon their lips because rarely was silver in their hands.

Their faces in repose were twisted as though in anger, only—it was not anger. It was the years of straining at loads too heavy for them which had lifted their upper lips to bare their teeth in a seeming snarl, and this labor had set deep wrinkles in the flesh about their eyes and their mouths. They themselves had no idea of what manner of men they were. One of them once, seeing himself in a mirror that passed on a van of household goods, had cried out, "There is an ugly fellow!" And when others laughed at him loudly he smiled painfully, never knowing at what they laughed, and looking about hastily to see if he had offended someone.

At home in the small hovels where they lived, around Wang Lung's hovel, heaped one upon another, the women sewed rags together to make a covering for the children they were forever breeding, and they snatched at bits of cabbage from farmers' fields and stole handfuls of rice from the grain markets, and gleaned the year round the grass on the hillsides; and at harvest they followed the reapers like fowls, their eyes piercing and sharp for every dropped grain or stalk. And through these huts passed children; they were born and dead and born again until neither mother or father knew how many had been born or had died, and scarcely knew even how many were living, thinking of them only as mouths to be fed.

Carson McCullers

Carson McCullers

(1917–1967)

"To me the most impressive aspect of *The Heart Is a Lonely Hunter* is the astonishing humanity that enables a white writer, for the first time in southern fiction, to handle Negro characters with as much ease and justice as those of her own race," wrote Richard Wright, author of *Native Son* and *Black Boy*, in 1940. Carson McCullers was just 23 years old when that book, her first, was published. It made her famous, and the plays and stories she wrote later helped seal her reputation as one of the finest fiction writers of the American South.

Lula Carson Smith was born in Columbus, Georgia. She dreamed of becoming a concert pianist. But when Carson was a high school senior, she contracted rheumatic fever, and amused herself by writing plays and stories. Her plans changed: she would be a writer when she grew up. After graduation, she moved to New York City to study creative writing at Columbia University. At 18, she met James Reeves McCullers, Jr., a friend of a friend. A year later, her first short story was published, and she began *The Heart Is a Lonely Hunter*, about a young woman and her relationships with a variety of characters in a southern town, including a deaf mute named Singer.

At 20, she married Reeves and they moved to Charlotte, North Carolina. There she finished her first novel, completed *Reflections in a Golden Eye*, and started *The Member of the Wedding*. In 1940, *The Heart Is a Lonely Hunter* was published to excellent critical reviews. McCullers, who fell ill—likely as a result of her earlier rheumatic fever—was now writing poetry. While visiting the Yaddo Artists' Colony, she wrote *The Ballad of the Sad Café* (1943), and filed for divorce from Reeves. They remarried five years later.

After suffering a stroke that left her partially paralyzed, McCullers attempted suicide. She recuperated in Nantucket, collaborating with playwright Tennessee Williams, a fellow southern writer, on a stage version of *The Member of the Wedding* (1951). The production was a critical success, but Carson's marriage was foundering again, and her husband committed suicide in 1953.

Plagued by illness and alcohol dependency, she threw herself into work, writing two more novels: *The Square Root of Wonderful* (1958) and *Clock Without Hands* (1961), the latter another observant chronicle of black and white life in a southern town. By 1962, McCullers was confined to a wheelchair. Her children's verse book, *Sweet as a Pickle, Clean as a Pig*, was published in 1964. After her death, McCuller's sister, Margarita Smith, edited a posthumous collection of her works, *The Mortgaged Heart*. In 1999, her unfinished autobiography, *Illumination and Night Glare*, was published. The title refers to the periods of happiness and depression that defined her life.

In this excerpt from The Heart Is a Lonely Hunter *(1940), Mick Kelly, a dreamy yet pragmatic young girl, escapes the torpor of her sleepy Southern town and her family's poverty by writing music, imagining the day when she might perform it for an appreciative audience.*

She had worked on music in this notebook all the winter. She quit studying school lessons at night so she could have more time to spend on music. Mostly she had written just little tunes—songs without any words and without even any bass notes to them. They were very short. But even if the tunes were only half a page long she gave them names and drew her initials underneath them. Nothing in this book was a real piece or a composition. They were just songs in her mind she wanted to remember. She named them how they reminded her—"Africa" and "A Big Fight" and "The Snowstorm."

She couldn't write the music just like it sounded in her mind. She had to thin it down to only a few notes; otherwise she got too mixed up to go further. There was so much she didn't know about how to write music. But maybe after she learned how to write these simple tunes fairly quick she could begin to put down the whole music in her mind.

In January she began a certain very wonderful piece called "This Thing I Want, I Know Not What." It was a beautiful and marvelous song—very slow and soft. At first she had started to write a poem along with it, but she couldn't think of ideas to fit the music. Also it was hard to get a word for the third line to rhyme what. This new song made her feel sad and excited and happy all at once. Music beautiful as this was hard to work on. Any song was hard to write. Something she could hum in two minutes meant a whole week's work before it was down in the notebook—after she had figured up the scale and the time and every note.

She had to concentrate hard and sing it many times. Her voice was always hoarse. Her Dad said this was because she had bawled so much when she was a baby. Her Dad would have to get up and walk with her every night when she was Ralph's age. The only thing would hush her, he always said, was for him to beat the coal scuttle with a poke and sing "Dixie."

She lay on her stomach on the cold floor and thought. Later on—when she was twenty—she would be a great world-famous composer. She would have a whole symphony orchestra and conduct all of her music herself. She would stand up on the platform in front of the big crowds of people. To conduct the orchestra she would wear either a real man's evening suit or else a red dress spangled with rhinestones. The curtains of the stage would be red velvet and M.K. would be printed on them in gold. Mister Singer would be there, and afterward they would go out and eat fried chicken. He would admire her and count her as his very best friend. George would bring up big wreaths of flowers to the stage. It would be in New York City or else in a foreign country. Famous people would point at her—Carole Lombard and Arturo Toscanini and Admiral Byrd.

And she could play the Beethoven symphony any time she wanted to. It was a queer thing about this music she had heard last autumn. The symphony stayed inside her always and grew little by little. The reason was this: the whole symphony was in her mind. It had to be. She had heard every note, and somewhere in the back of her mind the whole of the music was still there just as it had been played. But she could do nothing to bring it all out again. Except wait and be ready for the times when suddenly a new part came to her. Wait for it to grow like leaves grow slowly on the branches of a spring oak tree.

Adrienne Rich

(born 1929)

Her poems are elegant and truthful, while her politics reflect a spectrum of modern injustices and dislocations. Few contemporary poets have cast such a sharp yet empathetic eye on the human condition—particularly that of women—and spoken of it so eloquently, both in anger and in love. Turning from an Adrienne Rich poem to the world around us, things look more profound; senses are heightened. Such is the power of her writing.

Adrienne Cecile Rich was born in Baltimore, Maryland. Her mother was a musician who abandoned her career to raise her family. Her father, a physician and professor, encouraged his daughter to read and write poetry. Rich graduated from Radcliffe College in 1951, winning the prestigious Yale Younger Poets Prize for *A Change of World*, her first book. Two years later she married Alfred Conrad, a Harvard economist.

Rich gave birth to three sons. Early motherhood was difficult, for she was torn between a traditional woman's role and a longing for freedom. This conflict, she has noted, caused great guilt and confusion in the 50s and early 60s, when women did not speak openly about such feelings. Twenty years later, she would explore these emotions in a landmark book, *Of Woman Born: Motherhood as Experience and Institution* (1976).

In 1966, Rich and Conrad moved to New York City, where she taught college remedial English to nontraditional students. She produced several important books of poetry: *Necessities of Life* (1966), *Leaflets* (1969), and *The Will to Change* (1971). Feminist issues grew in significance. In the poem "Tear Gas," she writes, "The will to change begins in the body not in the mind / My politics is in my body."

As the world changed, so did Adrienne Rich, whose work chronicled the unfolding civil rights, antiwar, and women's movements. She wrote about human rights, sexual politics, racism, lesbian identity, and women's identity—her own as well as others'. She has taken up these issues in prose as well as in poetry. *On Lies, Secrets, and Silence* (1979) recounts her explorations of women's consciousness, including their relationships, their education, and the necessity of honor. "Honesty in women has not been considered important," she observes. "We have been depicted as generically whimsical, deceitful, subtle, vacillating. And we have been rewarded for lying."

When she received the National Book Award in 1974 for *Diving into the Wreck*, Rich accepted it with the other nominees, Alice Walker and Audre Lorde, in the name of all women who have been silenced. Since then she has been the recipient of a MacArthur Fellowship, the Dorothea Tanning Prize, and a Lannan Lifetime Achievement Award, among other honors. Her most recent books are *Arts of the Possible: Essays and Conversations,* and *Fox: Poems 1998–2001* (both Norton, 2001).

Here Rich lovingly and sympathetically acknowledges the everyday struggles of women, even as she champions the healing power of the poem itself. Weary mothers, adolescents, elderly, the disenfranchised, abused, and lonely—she reaches out to all in "(Dedications)" (1990–1991).

(Dedications)

I know you are reading this poem
late, before leaving your office
of the one intense yellow lamp-spot and the darkening window
in the lassitude of a building faded to quiet
long after rush-hour. I know you are reading this poem
standing up in a bookstore far from the ocean
on a grey day of early spring, faint flakes driven
across the plains' enormous spaces around you.
I know you are reading this poem
in a room where too much has happened for you to bear
where the bedclothes lie in stagnant coils on the bed
and the open valise speaks of flight

Adrienne Rich

but you cannot leave yet. I know you are reading this poem
as the underground train loses momentum and before running
                              up the stairs
toward a new kind of love
your life has never allowed.
I know you are reading this poem by the light
of the television screen where soundless images jerk and slide
while you wait for the newscast from the *intifada*.
I know you are reading this poem in a waiting-room
of eyes met and unmeeting, of identity with strangers.
I know you are reading this poem by fluorescent light
in the boredom and fatigue of the young who are counted out,
count themselves out, at too early an age. I know
you are reading this poem through your failing sight, the thick
lens enlarging these letters beyond all meaning yet you read on
because even the alphabet is precious.
I know you are reading this poem as you pace beside the stove
warming milk, a crying child on your shoulder, a book in your
                              hand
because life is short and you too are thirsty.
I know you are reading this poem which is not in your language
guessing at some words while others keep you reading
and I want to know which words they are.
I know you are reading this poem listening for something, torn
                       between bitterness and hope
turning back once again to the task you cannot refuse.
I know you are reading this poem because there is nothing else
                              left to read
there where you have landed, stripped as you are.

This excerpt from Twenty-One Love Poems *(1978), an exquisitely rendered moment of joy, mature but still euphoric—in this case, sprung from the poet's newfound passion for a woman—is leavened by the wisdom of age and experience.*

XII

Sleeping, turning in turn like planets
rotating in their midnight meadow:
a touch is enough to let us know
we're not alone in the universe, even in sleep:
the dream-ghosts of two worlds
walking their ghost-towns, almost address each other.
I've wakened to your muttered words
spoken light- or dark-years away
as if my own voice had spoken.
But we have different voices, even in sleep,
and our bodies, so alike, are yet so different
and the past echoing through our bloodstreams
is freighted with different language, different meanings—
though in any chronicle of the world we share
it could be written with new meaning
we were two lovers of one gender,
we were two women of one generation.

Joyce Carol Oates

(born 1938)

"To write is to invade another's space, if only to memorialize it," remarked Joyce Carol Oates in a *New York Times* column, "Writers on Writing." As this contemporary American author has "invaded" thousands of places, familiar and unfamiliar, her enormous body of work has increased accordingly. She is often called America's most prolific writer.

Oates' literary output is daunting both for its sheer volume and for its wide range of styles and subjects. It includes sweeping Gothic tales (*Bellefleur*, 1980, *My Heart Laid Bare* 1998), family chronicles (*You Must Remember This*, 1989, *We Were the Mulvaneys*, 1996), taut short stories charged with violence, essays, fictional biographies (*Blonde*, an intimate look at Marilyn Monroe, 2000), evocative poetry, plays, stories about women (*Solstice*, 1985, and *Marya: A Life*, 1986) and under the pseudonym Rosamond Smith, a series of suspense novels. She has written essays on William Shakespeare, Stephen King, boxer Mike Tyson, and poet Sylvia Plath. In recent years, she has issued books at the rate of two a year.

Oates was born in rural Lockport, New York. Her earliest memories are of rambles through the countryside, making up stories in her head. She created lengthy "novels," composed of drawings and scribbles, before she was old enough to read or write, and was an avid storyteller. Given a typewriter at fourteen, her fate seemed determined. Joyce immediately began writing stories and novels. While attending Syracuse University, her work was first published when she won a fiction contest sponsored by *Mademoiselle* magazine. She began contributing short stories to literary magazines and reviews.

Oates received a master's degree in English from the University of Wisconsin, where she met Raymond Smith, her future husband. They married and moved to Detroit. The

Joyce Carol Oates

violent nature of that city in the mid-60s, she has said, profoundly influenced her work, particularly her acclaimed early novel *them* (1969). *By the North Gate*, Oates' first collection of stories, was published in 1963. She continued to write while she and Smith taught at the University of Windsor, just over the border in Canada. Together they established the *Ontario Review*, a distinguished literary journal, in 1974.

In 1978, Oates and Smith moved to Princeton, New Jersey, where they began publishing books under the Ontario Review Press imprint in 1980. Oates is a professor of creative writing at Princeton University. She has been nominated for a PEN/Faulkner Award and a Pulitzer Prize, and has won numerous literary awards and honors. No other writer, male or female, has consistently shown the energy and eye for detail that informs Joyce Carol Oates' work. Her mission, it seems, is to chronicle life in all its guises—the everyday, the fantastic, the romantic, the harrowing—and she shows no signs of ceasing.

Most readers think of Oates primarily as a novelist and essayist, but her mastery extends to verse. In this lovely, moving poem, poignant images of childhood Christmases are contrasted with the reality of adults who create and perpetuate those memorable holiday fantasies.

Christmas: The House Adrift in a Wide White Ocean of Snow

Black December is a ditch winking overhead
but here beneath your parents' roof the piecrust faces
are dimpled by forks
and the clock faces are round and smooth as buttons.
This is the season of waiting and of expectation
and of hunger keenly roused to be satisfied.
This is the season of the miraculous birth,
the oldest story,
these years,
centuries—
the fresh-trimmed spruce bristling to the ceiling
smelling of cold, of night, of forests wild and tamed
as forests in a child's picture book.
The splendid tree is balanced in a shallow tin of water
looking as if it would live forever—

green-spicy, sharp-needled—
and such tinsel, such trinkets ablaze
on the boughs, a glass-glitter
of icicles, angel's hair,
strings of colored lights plugged to a socket!
And beneath the tree presents wrapped in shiny paper,
satiny bows, gifts heaped upon gifts—
a child's fever-dream spilled on the carpet.
Outside, snow flying like white horses' manes and tails,
inside cookies that are stars, hearts, diamonds,
the smell of a turkey roasting slow in its fat.
There are stories children are not told
of grandmothers dying in secret of their hearts
or of cancer shopping for months for this season—
the costly boxed gifts that are love, the stiff silver paper
that is love, all the effort of joy, love—
torn open too quickly by a child's fingers.
And there suddenly is your father
young again—
entering the kitchen, the wind behind him,
snow melting in his wild dark hair,
a carton of presents in his arms.
From what and to what could this world be redeemed?
—is not a child's question.
You are sitting at the long table with the others.
Those years. The roof weighted with snow. Candle flames,
the smell of red wax, O take and eat, the crock tells
its small rounded time again
and again, again—
this is all there is and this is everything.
The miraculous birth is your own.

Margaret Atwood

(born 1939)

Canada's most important contemporary writer, Margaret Atwood appeals to both the reader of popular fiction and the connoisseur of fine literature. Her work, which includes such novels as *The Handmaid's Tale* (1986), *Alias Grace* (1996), and *The Robber Bride* (1993), short stories, and poetry, is suffused with realism, truth, texture, humor, and tragedy. In fiction, she fearlessly explores such facets of modern life as domestic violence, eating disorders, and the conflicting roles of women in society. In literary criticism and essays, such as *Strange Things: The Malevolent North in Canadian Literature* (1995), she reveals herself to be a staunch Canadian nationalist.

Margaret Eleanor Atwood was born in Ottowa, Ontario. Her father, an entomologist, brought his family to live in a primitive cabin in the woods for much of her childhood. Margaret turned to books for company. It became clear that writing would be her life's work, though her parents had encouraged her to study botany, believing it ensured a better chance for supporting herself. She graduated Victoria College at the University of Toronto in 1961, and received a master's degree from Radcliffe College in Cambridge, Massachusetts. Atwood published her first book of poems herself, literally: she carefully hand-set the type on a vintage printing press, and sold the volumes for fifty cents apiece.

Soon her poetry captured the attention of major publishers, and was published in *The Circle Game* (1967), *The Animals in That Country* (1968), and *The Journals of Susanna Moodie* (1970), the latter inspired by journals of an upper-class English woman who moved to Canada with her family in 1832. *The Edible Woman* (1969) was Atwood's first novel, an ironic feminist look at a young woman who becomes unable to eat after becoming engaged.

Margaret Atwood

Atwood has taught English at universities in Vancouver, Montreal, and Toronto. She holds a number of honorary college degrees and has received dozens of awards for her writing. In 2000, she published what may be her most ambitious work of fiction to date: *The Blind Assassin*, a story about two sisters that incorporates a novel-within-a-novel written by one sister, who has died under mysterious circumstances.

Atwood enthusiasts breathlessly await each new publication, and the devotion of some fans to their favorite writer has been described as cult-like. On the other hand, the Margaret Atwood Society, an international association affiliated with the Modern Language Association, produces a biannual newsletter and is dedicated to scholarly study of her writing. She is a popular author among members of private book clubs, where her characters and themes are discussed at length. In interviews, Atwood declines to interpret her work, leaving that to the discretion of the reader.

In 1975, she married the Canadian novelist Graeme Gibson. They have three grown children, and live in Toronto.

The Robber Bride (1993) is a quintessential Atwood tale that combines intrigue, drama, ironic humor, and sexual politics. Here, a mysterious, almost mythical character makes an unexpected appearance, and things are never the same afterward.

One evening Zenia appears at their door. She knocks like anybody else and Tony opens, thinking it is a Girl Guide selling cookies, or else the Jehovah's Witnesses. When she sees Zenia standing there she can't think of what to say. She's holding a skewer in her hand, with chunks of lamb and tomato and green pepper threaded onto it, and for an instant she has a vision of herself plunging the skewer into Zenia, into where her heart should be, but she doesn't do this. She just stands there with her mouth open, and Zenia smiles at her and says, "Tony darling, it was such work to track you down!" and laughs with her white teeth. She's thinner now, and even more sophisticated. She's wearing a black miniskirt, a black shawl with jet beading and long silken fringes, fishnet tights, and knee-high lace-up highheeled boots.

"Come in," says Tony, motioning with her skewer. Lamb blood drips onto the floor.

"Who is it?" calls West from the living room, where he's playing Purcell on the spinet. He likes to play while Tony is making dinner: it's one of their little rituals.

Nobody, Tony wants to say. *They had the wrong address. They went away.* She wants to thrust her hands at Zenia, push her back, slam the door. But Zenia is already over the threshold.

"West! My God!" she says, striding into the living room, holding out her arms to him. "Long time no see!" West can't believe it. His eyes behind his rimless glasses are the shocked eyes of a burned baby, the amazed eyes of an interstellar traveller. He doesn't get up, he doesn't move. Zenia takes his upturned face in her two hands and kisses him twice, once on each cheek, and then a third time on the forehead. The fringes of her shawl caress him, his mouth is level with her chest. "It's so good to see old friends," says Zenia, breathing out.

Somehow or other she ends up staying for dinner, because who are Tony and West to hold grudges, and what is there to hold them about anyway? Wasn't it Zenia's defection that brought them together? And aren't they touchingly happy? Zenia tells them they are. They're just like a couple of kids, she says, kids on one long picnic, playing sand castles at the beach. So darling! She says she's delighted to see it. Then she sighs, implying that life has not treated her as well as it's been treating them. But then, she hasn't had their advantages. She's lived on the edges, out there where it's dark and sharp and there are scarcities. She's had to forage.

Where has she been? Well, Europe, she says, gesturing towards a higher, a deeper culture; and the States, where the big folks play; and the Middle East. (With a wave of her hand she invokes deserts, date palms, mystic knowledge, and better shish kebab than anything capable of being grilled in Tony's wee Canadian oven.) She avoids saying what she's been doing in these places. This and that, she says. She laughs, and says she has a short attention span.

About the money she made off with she tactfully says nothing, and Tony decides that it would be parochial of her to bring it up. Zenia does say, "Oh, there's your wonderful lute, I always loved it," as if she

has no memory whatsoever of her own kidnapping of this instrument. West seems to have no memory of it either. At Zenia's request he plays a few of the old songs; though he doesn't do folksongs much any more, he says. By now he's into a cross-cultural study of polyphonal chants.

No memory, no memory. Does nobody but Tony have any memory at all? Apparently not; or rather West has no memory, and Zenia's is highly selective. She gives little nudges, little hints, and assumes a rueful expression: she has regrets, is what she implies, but she has sacrificed her own happiness for that of West. Hearth and home are what he needs, not a feckless, mossless rover like Zenia, and Tony is such a busy little housewife—isn't this cunning food! West is where he belongs: like a houseplant in the right window, just look how he's flourishing! "You two are so lucky," she whispers to Tony, a mournful catch in her voice. West overhears, as he is meant to.

"Where are you staying?" Tony asks politely, meaning, when are you leaving.

"Oh, you know," says Zenia with a shrug. "Here and there. I live from hand to mouth—or from feast to famine. Just like the old days, remember, West? Remember our feasts?" She's eating a Viennese chocolate, from a box West brought home to surprise Tony. He often brings her little treats, little atonements for the part of himself he's unable to give her. Zenia licks the dark chocolate from her fingers, one by one, gazing at West from between her eyelashes. "Delicious," she says richly.

Tony can't believe that West doesn't see through all this, this blandishment and prestidigitation, but he doesn't. He has a blind spot: his blind spot is Zenia's unhappiness. Or else her body. Men, thinks Tony with new bitterness, can't seem to tell one from the other.

A few days after that, West comes home later than usual. "I took Zenia out for a beer," he tells Tony. He has the air of a man who is being scrupulously honest even though he's been tempted not to be. "She's having a rough time. She's a very vulnerable person. I'm quite worried about her."

Vulnerable? Where did West pick up that word?

Tony thinks Zenia is about as vulnerable as a cement block, but she doesn't say so. Instead she says something almost as bad. "I suppose she wants some money."

West looks hurt. "Why don't you like her?" he asks. "You used to be such good friends. She's noticed, you know. She's upset about it."

"Because of what she did to *you*," says Tony indignantly. "That's why I don't like her!"

West is puzzled. "What did she do to me?" he asks. He really doesn't know.

ACKNOWLEDGMENTS

EMILY DICKINSON: Reprinted by permission of the publishers and the Trustees of Amherst College from *The Poems of Emily Dickinson*, Thomas H. Johnson, ed., Cambridge, Mass.: The Belknap Press of Harvard University Press, Copyright © 1951, 1955, 1979 by the President and Fellows of Harvard College.

KATE CHOPIN: Art reference: © Missouri Historical Society, St. Louis.

COLETTE: Excerpt from *The Blue Lantern* by Colette, translated by Roger Senhouse. Translation copyright © 1963 by Farrar, Straus & Giroux, Inc. "The Hand" from *The Collected Stories of Colette* edited by Robert Phelps, and translated by Matthew Ward. Translation copyright © 1983 by Farrar, Straus & Giroux, Inc. Art reference: Roger Viollet Documentation Photographique.

GERTRUDE STEIN: From *Selected Writings of Gertrude Stein* by Gertrude Stein, edited by Carl Van Vechten, copyright © 1946 by Random House, Inc. From *Autobiography of Alice B. Toklas* by Gertrude Stein, copyright © 1933 and renewed 1961 by Alice B. Toklas. Reprinted by permission of Random House, Inc. and the Estate of Gertrude Stein.

VIRGINIA WOOLF: Excerpt from *A Room of One's Own* by Virginia Woolf, copyright © 1929 by Harcourt, Inc. and renewed 1957 by Leonard Woolf, reprinted by permission of the publisher and by The Society of Authors. Excerpt from *The Second Common Reader* by Virginia Woolf, copyright © 1932 by Harcourt, Inc. and renewed 1960 by Leonard Woolf, reprinted by permission of the publisher and by The Society of Authors. Art reference: Hulton Deutsch Collection Limited.

ISAK DINESEN: From *Out of Africa* by Isak Dinesen, copyright © 1937 by Random House, Inc. and renewed 1965 by Rungstedlundfonden. Used by permission of Random House, Inc. and The Rungstedlund Foundation. Art reference: Camera Press Ltd.

MARIANNE MOORE: Reprinted with the permission of Scribner, a Division of Simon & Schuster, Inc. and Faber and Faber Ltd. from *Collected Poems* by Marianne Moore. Copyright © 1935 by Marianne Moore and renewed 1963 by Marianne Moore and T.S. Eliot. Art reference: Camera Press Ltd.

EDITH SITWELL: From *Collected Poems* by Edith Sitwell, published by Sinclair Stevenson. Reprinted by permission of David Higham Associates.

KATHERINE MANSFIELD: Art reference: Camera Press Ltd.

SIMONE DE BEAUVOIR: From *The Woman Destroyed* by Simone de Beauvoir, copyright © 1969 by Collins Publishers, and G.P. Putnam's Sons. Used by permission of Pantheon Books, a division of Random House, Inc, and HarperCollins Publishers Ltd. Art reference: © Gisèle Freund/ Agency Nina Beskow.

EUDORA WELTY: From *The Optimist's Daughter* by Eudora Welty, copyright © 1968, 1972, by Eudora Welty. Used by permission of Random House, Inc. and Russell & Volkening. Art reference: Thomas Victor/TimePix.

DORIS LESSING: From *The Summer Before the Dark* by Doris Lessing, copyright © 1973 by Doris Lessing. Used by permission of Alfred A. Knopf, a division of Random House, Inc. Reprinted by kind permission of Jonathan Clowes Ltd., London, on behalf of Peter Lessing. Art reference: Camera Press Ltd.

NADINE GORDIMER: "Something Out There," copyright © 1984 by Nadine Gordimer, from *Something Out There* by Nadine Gordimer. Used by Permission of Viking Penguin, a division of Penguin Putnam Inc., Penguin Books Canada Limited, and A.P. Watt Ltd. on behalf of Nadine Gordimer. Art reference: Frank Spooner Pictures Ltd. From *Something Out There* by Nadine Gordimer. Copyright © 1984 Felix Licensing B.V. Reprinted by Permission of Penguin Books Canada Limited.

FLANNERY O'CONNOR: Excerpt from "Everything That Rises Must Converge" from *The Complete Stories* by Flannery O'Connor. Copyright © 1961, 1965, 1971 by the Estate of Mary Flannery O'Connor. Reprinted by permission of Farrar, Straus & Giroux, Inc. and Harold Matson Co. Art reference: Illustration based on photo © by Joe McTyre/*Atlanta Journal-Constitution*.

URSULA K. LE GUIN: Copyright © 1969 by Ursula K. Le Guin, from *The Left Hand of Darkness*; reprinted by permission of the author and the author's agents, the Virginia Kidd Agency, Inc. Art reference: Camera Press Ltd.

TONI MORRISON: Reprinted by permission of International Creative Management, Inc. Copyright © 1977 Toni Morrison. Art reference: Frank Spooner Pictures Ltd.

EDNA O'BRIEN: Excerpt from *The Country Girls Trilogy* by Edna O'Brien. Copyright © 1960, renewed 1988 by Edna O'Brien. Reprinted by permission of Farrar, Straus and Giroux, Inc. and David Godwin Associates.

GEORGE SAND: Reprinted with permission from Siân Miles' translation of *Marianne* by George Sand, Copyright © 1987 by Siân Miles, published by Carroll & Graf Publishers, Inc., New York, NY. Art reference: © Corbis-Bettmann.

CHARLOTTE BRONTË: Art reference: © Corbis-Bettmann.